GREAT BALLS OF FUR

"Shauna"

GREAT BALLS
of
FUR

Life with Newfoundlands
and Other Critters

NITA JAGER
Illustrated by Claire Carr

FITHIAN PRESS
SANTA BARBARA
1992

Design and typography by Jim Cook
Cover illustration: Pandaga's Chanson de la Mer "Shauna" by Deborah Fetcinko

LIBRARY OF CONGRESS CATALOGING-IN-PUBLICATION DATA
Jager, Nita
    Great balls of fur: life with Newfoundlands and other critters/
Nita Jager.
        p.   cm.
    ISBN 1-56474-021-8
    1. Newfoundland dog—Anecdotes. 2. Pets—Anecdotes.
3. Jager, Nita. I. Title.
SF429.N4J34   1992   92-1339
636.7'3—dc20   CIP

These stories are dedicated
to the precious memory of
Ganshalom's Shachor Kasam,
the most beloved and the
most sorely missed
of all the Newfoundlands
I have known and cherished.

Contents

Preface

This is a collection of true stories, mostly about four people and their pets. Occasionally the order of events has been altered, or other minor adjustments made, to make the stories more readable—less cluttered—than real life, but the facts are true to the best of my ability to remember and recount them. This point is being made by way of apology to anyone whose recollection might differ from mine and also to preclude the possibility that anyone might think I have embroidered the accounts to enhance the dogs' personalities or actions. The latter is not only untrue, it would be wholly unnecessary. If the dogs seem larger than life, it is because they are, or were. Everyone who has shared life with a Newfoundland knows there is no need to glorify these marvelous creatures. They deserve every conceivable accolade one can think to bestow upon them.

Without those very special Newfies, and other assorted pets, there could, of course, have been no such book as this. But, without the encouragement and help of some very special people there still would not have been. If there is credit to be meted out, it must be shared by my ever-supportive husband and daughters plus many other dear friends.

Special thanks are extended to Claire Carr, whose charming drawings do much to breathe life into my stories. Her knowledge of Newfoundlands—and her deep love for them—are as apparent as is her skill with pen and ink. I am also grateful to Deborah Fetcinko for permission to include her drawing of my current Newfoundland, Shauna; and to Jacqueline Brellochs, Shauna's breeder and previous owner, who not only had the drawing done but had first produced the dog.

A generous portion of credit must go to Bobbie Taylor, who managed to do what not one other person I know of could do—decipher and transcribe into readable type the appalling longhand scrawl in which all the following words were put onto paper by me.

—N. J.

Seattle, Washington
1992

GREAT BALLS
of
FUR

Without Regard to Color, Sex—

People who have Newfoundland dogs are exposed to some fascinating quirks of human nature, especially if they take their dogs to public places. For one thing, some folks just hate to admit they don't know the answer to a question, especially when it is put to them by someone in whose eyes they wish to appear cool and savvy.

> *Honey, what kind of dog is that?*
> > *A Saint Bernard.*
> *I never saw a black one before.*
> > *Oh, yes, lots of them are black.*
> *Daddy, could we have a dog like that?*
> > *Lord, no—he would eat us out of house and home.*

That latter was spoken in our hearing once by a man leading a setter-type mixed breed that may well have normally consumed twice what an adult Newfie does.

Early in the game a Newf owner is tempted to stop such passersby and set the record straight. It usually is not worth the effort; many people just do not want to be confused by the facts.

Sometimes, however, the owner is confronted directly and cannot gracefully escape, as happened to our daughter, Holly, one day when she walked along a beach with Emily, her caramel-colored Newfie. A stranger stopped her to ask about Emily's ancestry. Holly replied "Newfoundland." The man said "And what else?" Told that the dog is a purebred, he replied "Oh, no—Newfoundlands are never brown—he may be *part* Newfoundland, but he has to be part something else."

The truth, of course, is that there are brown Newfoundlands (but no black Saint Bernards), and Emily is one. There are also gray Newfs and black-and-white ones, the latter called Landseers for the painter who made them famous. In fact, because there are fewer of the nonblacks, they are especially prized by many and tend to fetch premium prices.

The truth is also that Emily is a "she," not a "he." It is amazing how many people assume that *every* large dog is a "he." (Toy poodles and powder-puff Maltese are probably always "shes.") More amazing: How do they think babies are ever born to any but middle-sized breeds?

Certainly, anyone not involved with a breed can readily be excused for not knowing the ins and outs of acceptable colors, coat types, and such (though perhaps less easily excused for being so sure they *do* know), and sex is not easily discernible on long-haired dogs, even by knowledgeable people. After all, in these days of unisex haircuts and clothing, most human parents have learned to take with a measure of humor such comments as "She's a little doll" in reference to their bouncing Brucie or "Isn't he a bruiser?" as little Gloria is chucked under the chin.

Still, the lack of recognition of each individual's uniqueness can be strangely upsetting. Some such innocuous question as "How do you tell them apart?—they look *exactly* alike!" whether tossed at a mother of twins or an owner of two or more black Newfoundlands, may open a flood-gate of response. Even after years of exposure, we sometimes find ourselves taking the bait thus proffered and launching into a lengthy catalogue of the endless differences—in size, eye color, coat, facial shape, set of ears, expression, movement, and on and on and on—between our several Newfs. To us, each is so unlike the others, so distinctly and in such very special ways utterly himself or herself, that we are likely to be quite impatient with what we used to deem the novice's lack of the most rudimentary powers of observation.

Pride, as we would have done well to remember, goeth before a fall, and we got our comeuppance once in a scary way. We had all been out of town, and, as usual in those days, had left our three Newfies at a boarding kennel. The kennel was a superb one, near our home, owned by friends who knew and loved dogs, and run with impeccable efficiency. We never had the slightest concern about the well-being of our "babies" left there. Somewhat lonely for us, they might be—although the excitement of being near other dogs and the on-going activities of a busy kennel may have been more fun than the expectable routine of home. We thought what they probably missed most was their togetherness with each other.

In a still earlier episode, that concern had nearly caused us to become persona non grata with the kennel owners and involved our huge male, Shalom, who had developed over-protective attitudes about Holly's young undersized bitch, 'Sicha. Even the slightest threat to 'Sicha's safety would prompt him to any action necessary to put himself between her and the perceived danger. More than once he had bulldozed his way through fences and other supposedly impregnable barriers to follow her when she pulled one of her Houdini-style escapes. Although we were aware that even Shalom could not breach the concrete-footed, chain-link fencing that bounded the runs at the boarding kennel, we worried that he would injure himself in the attempt, if he and 'Sicha were separated, with dozens of other strange dogs in close proximity to her. So we begged our friend to house Shalom and 'Sicha together. Both the indoor enclosures for large dogs and the outdoor runs to which each was connected were quite roomy and could easily accommodate even two Newfoundlands.

The kennel owner was, however, adamant. No way he would house two animals together regardless of their friendship or their home conditions. "Pets behave differently away from home," he explained for the *n*th time. "I have seen the best of friends, used to sharing food dishes and sleeping blankets at home, go at each other's throats when plunked down in the unfamiliar and some-times threatening environment of a kennel. I won't take the risk."

"But no Newf goes at *any* throat, *ever—you* know that," we countered, exaggerating only slightly. "And," we continued, "you know these two dogs personally. Marshmallows, both of them." Sensing he was close to reconsidering, we pushed our advantage, stressing the risk we saw to Shalom (of whom our friend was extraordinarily fond) if they were separated, and even offering to sign a paper assuming responsibility if any difficulties arose from housing them together. Our final sally put the frosting on the cake—for he is a frugal person who enjoys a dollar as much as anyone—and we pointed out that we would pay the usual rate for both, but he would have an extra slot to rent to someone else.

At last he yielded, although still reluctantly. That was very nearly the last time he let one of our dogs on his property at all! The first two days we were gone, all was fine, he later told us. On the third day, near-tragedy occurred in a most bizarre fashion. That morn-ing, kennel attendants went through the building as usual and pulled the chains that lifted the connecting doors between inside cages and outside runs. As was typical, most dogs raced outside the moment they could. Our two kids were also ready for an outdoor romp, but 'Sicha—so much smaller, younger, and quicker than Shalom—was through the door and had galloped to the end of the run and back before Shalom lumbered to his feet and gathered his massive self to follow. He plunged outward through the door just as 'Sicha, probably barreling back to tell him what a glorious morning it was, shot into the opening from the other direction. They stuck. They tried to go forward and could not. They tried to back up, and their shoulders locked. They panicked. And so did all the people present.

We can only imagine the frantic, chaotic events of the next minutes. Our friend became well-nigh incoherent trying to describe them. All we learned was that, in desperation, he and his helpers ripped out half the wall in that section of the kennel to free our kids. A careful examination of both animals by him showed no damage to either dog beyond the probability of a few bruises. And, although carpenters could restore the wall with relative ease, our friend swore that nothing could repair the damage to his nerves. He also could not resist mentioning that, instead of saving him money, the episode cost him: not only did he have to use two spaces for our dogs from then on, but the one they had been in was out of commission for a week while repairs were done. Luckily for us, he was not one to hold a grudge, and our friendship endured the test.

Then came the second test, with an identity twist, a few years later. Shalom was long gone from this world, and 'Sicha's escape art had finally brought about her deportation to more secure quarters elsewhere, but we had three adult Newfs to be boarded while Don, Holly, and I were on vacation. One was Holly's dog, Melech, a son of 'Sicha; another was my especially beloved Kasam; the third was a young bitch named Tari. We got home from our trip toward evening, and a call to the boarding kennel let us know all three dogs were okay and could be picked up that day if we could get there within a few minutes, as the kennel was about to close for the night. We were all busy, so Holly was elected to go alone in the Jeep wagon and collect the whole gang at once. When she got back, she was ruffled and breathless, complaining of the dogs' awful behavior in the car. She said they were roughhousing and tumbling so around the back she could hardly keep the car in the road—behavior far different from their usual sedate riding postures—and that she'd also had a terrible time getting them out of the car and herded through the gate into the big pen at home. She mentioned that Melech had been the worst, climbing all over the girls, and she wondered if one of them might be coming in heat. I thought it a possible explanation, but since it was really too early for either of them to be due, it seemed more likely that they were just excited to be together again after the long separation.

A look out the windows confirmed that they were still behaving wildly—leaping, tumbling about, chasing each other—so it seemed best for me to stop what I was doing long enough to get them calmed down. When I opened the door to the main dog room, they came roaring in like supercharged bulls with such exuberance that I was temporarily hemmed in by a plunging, leaping mass of black fur and red tongues. Pushing them off, trying to pet them, and speaking their names, I managed to restore a bit of order, but they were still milling about and nudging one another far more than usual. So I trotted out my firmest voice and told each one to "Sit! Melech," "Sit, 'Sam," "Sit! Tari," "*No*, 'Sam, sit!!," "Melech, you *sit!* and *stay!*" As I went from one to another—and they kept shifting places—I called them half the time by the wrong names, and we were all getting utterly confused. But no wonder! It finally dawned on me, as I was in the process of forcibly planting a male Newfoundland into the sit position, that *another* male was standing right in front of me. Sure enough, there were two males and one female, not the two bitches and one male that belonged to us. "Holly," I bellowed. "Come here. Something is wrong. We have two males."

It turned out we had our Melech (male), and our Tari (female), and another, unknown, male. Belonging to whom? I didn't know and, at that moment, quite selfishly didn't care. All I did care was that one of our dogs—no, not "one" of our dogs but my most special, most cherished 'Sam!—was missing. How could it be? *Where* was she? I couldn't believe such a terrible thing could be happening.

And I was furious. At the kennel personnel (how stupid!) and with Holly. How could she have accepted a strange dog—and *in place* of my 'Sam?? Then I realized—oh, how sheepishly—how long I had watched the dogs out the window and then tried to sort out bodies downstairs before *I* noticed that 'Sam was missing. Where had my powers of discernment been? Could I be sure I would have noticed the individuals better and caught the mistake immediately if I had been the one collecting them? It was a humbling experience.

There was little time to dwell on that at the moment. 'Sam had to be found. A few calls back and forth to the kennel and the story was sorted out. In addition to our three, one other Newfoundland had been boarded at the kennel (the unknown male we now had), and his owners had called for him earlier that afternoon. A newly hired kennel attendant had given them my 'Sammy. Several hours before! Yet, they had only discovered the error when they got the call from the kennel owner. Soon they were on their way back with her, and we were loading the extra male we had in our car.

The switch was soon accomplished—never did I hug 'Sam so vigorously!—and all was once again quiet at our house. Only then did it dawn on us what a testimonial to Newfoundland temperament we had witnessed. With what vigor and sternness I had pulled and pushed and physically downed the original milling crowd, of which one was an adult male Newfoundland I had never seen before. Nor he, me. And to realize that Melech had accepted with benevolence a strange male, herded first into his (Melech's) car, then into *his* pen, and *his* house—with *his* female! Excitement, but totally devoid of aggression, had been the response of all three. Marshmallows all.

And it *is* difficult to tell one marshmallow from another.

Sticks and Stones—and Rye Bread

Our Newfoundland dog, Kasam, had an insatiable and totally uncontrollable appetite. For food, yes, but for anything else she could swallow, which list eventually included a lot of weird items, some dangerous, others just funny. It was not always so. In her puppyhood, 'Sam had to be coaxed to eat, stepping back from competition with her littermates at the food dish and more than willing to forego the comforts of a full belly for those of human caresses. When she was started on the steroid drugs that were to be a part of her life forevermore, the coin flipped, and even love (or the withholding of it in the form of disapproval) usually failed to distract or deter her from the urge to consume. Shortly after the steroid therapy was begun and the list of things she was getting into included potentially toxic substances (entire bars of soap vanished from the sink and even the shower where she had to climb in and stand on hind legs to reach it), and other no-nos such as sticks and bark from shrubs in the exercise yard that splintered and caught in her throat, we confined her to the maximum-security pen—for her own safety.

That small enclosure, intended for bitches in heat and litters of puppies, was designed to prevent any creature (without wings) from getting in or out. It was austere to say the least. Ten-foot high redwood planks, backed with wire livestock fencing, were set six inches below ground. Large broken stones made a bed about four inches deep in the pen and were topped with smaller gravel. No grass, shrubs, or trees were in or near the pen. A redwood-in-stone sill overlapped the bottom of the gate. Gate latches were tight and used in pairs, one outside, one inside. The adjoining puppy room was as bare and protected: cement-covered walls, concrete floor, metal-sheathed door, and iron bars across the window.

Even in the "bitch prison," 'Sammy's mouth was almost the end of her. She ate the only available material—gravel. Talk about heavy, indigestible meals! Worse, though, the gravel was of a shale-type stone that, when chewed, separated into layers and flakes, some as sharp as razors. She had done her snacking on the sly, so when bloody stools appeared, we had no idea of the cause. Neither did Dr. Scott, a resident in allergies and dermatitis at the Cornell veterinary clinic, under whose care she had been for several months. He and I stared as, in the course of a rectal examination to try to determine the cause of the trouble, he began extracting bits and pieces of stone. Farther back, he found larger masses of the shale, imbedded in the intestinal lining and mixed with blood. The removal process was a long and tedious job. Dr. Scott did not appear terribly taken with my humor when, at one point, I asked him whether his momma knew she raised him and saw him off to eight years of college so he could learn to pick rocks out of a dog's rear.

So much for maximum security pens. Most of the rest of 'Sammy's life was spent indoors and almost always within sight of one of us. She was never left alone; when we both had to leave the house, she went in the car with one of us, or both. Many hours she spent in the back of the station wagon when we went to dinner, to a play, to visit friends, to run errands, to shop, to visit a doctor. It was the one place where her appetite appeared to sleep, and she was out of harm's way, even when left alone.

Kept as she was under constant surveillance, 'Sammy's forbidden-fruit experiences became increasingly rare, but never extinct.

A near-repeat of the gravel-eating episode occurred years later when we were having some remodeling done. With the house in a state of utter chaos, she escaped our vigilance one evening long enough to eat nearly six pounds of broken plaster. When the "treat" proved too much for even her cast-iron insides and she brought it back up, we couldn't believe what we were seeing. Then we couldn't believe the quantity, so we swept it into a dustpan and weighed it. A few days later, when another wall came down, we caught her in the act of gobbling up more.

Some of 'Sammy's eating adventures were amusing—though not always so at the time. One favorite involves a loaf of rye bread. After she was widowed, my mother-in-law, a dyed-in-the-wool New Yorker, reluctantly agreed to move west to be close to us, her only remaining family. It's not easy to change locale and habits after a lifetime, and food proved to be one of her major hurdles. I am convinced that even identical items, packaged differently, would have failed to please her. One very important item in her diet was bread—the Jewish rye she'd purchased for years at her neighborhood Brooklyn bakery. After months of trying breads from everywhere in Seattle, my husband found a Jewish rye she did like. Unfortunately, it was not available in the city; to get it, he had to drive across town and over the bridge to Bellevue, a time-consuming trip. We liked the bread too, so when he went he would get several loaves which I froze so we could have it often.

My mother-in-law, however, accustomed to doing her food-shopping daily in New York, distrusted all frozen food and thought that even to chill bread by putting it in the refrigerator was to render it inedible. Sometimes, in an effort to assuage some of her homesickness, Don would make a special trip just to get her a loaf of the rye bread. One afternoon, having done so, he had to delay delivering it until the next morning. I tucked my loaves in the freezer and started to put hers in the refrigerator for overnight safekeeping when my husband cautioned me not to. Mindful of the need to make it inaccessible to 'Sammy we settled for putting it in a high kitchen cupboard.

Don dressed for work the next day, ate breakfast, put his brief-case on the table by the front door, and only then, took out the bread for his mother. Remembering at the last minute some needed item in the bedroom, he set the bread on the briefcase and disappeared for what we both swore could not have exceeded two minutes. I was in the kitchen. He called goodbye, then turned back and asked where I'd put the bread. I hadn't touched it.

It was gone. Neatly. Not a crumb. We did find a few strips of the plastic bag and the twist-tie on the floor in the hall. We looked at each other and at the dog, lying nearby, and knew that calm and innocent expression belied a tummy full of two pounds of rye bread.

Don exploded. He had *promised* his mother a loaf of her favorite bread. He had arranged his schedule to get it and now to deliver it as well. Unable to face her disappointment he delved into the freezer and hauled out one of our loaves. Hard as a rock, of course. And this was winter.

All the way across town to her house, (he told me) he drove with one hand, holding the bread with the other in front of the car heater vent, turning and squeezing it to hasten the thawing process, slowing to a crawl the last mile to make sure it was ready.

The last laugh was still to come, and it was not Don's. When he gave the loaf to his mother, she looked in dismay at the size and announced that, since she had other bread started, she thought she'd just put this in the freezer for later!

It seems someone—not her son and certainly not her daughter-in-law—had convinced her that bread freezes very well. That loaf apparently froze well *twice*, because she told him later it was quite delicious.

'Sammy thought hers was too.

Gung Ho to Go

Newfoundland dogs are great travelers. It doesn't seem possible that something in the genes could account for their love of *going,* yet they all seem ready at all times to hop in and take off. Their desire not to be left behind is certainly a motivation—one shared by many pets of all breeds. But while some (of other breeds) that beg so hard to be taken are obviously miserable when they get their wish—nervously skittering to and fro, whining and whimpering, shivering and wild-eyed, and sometimes tossing their breakfasts to boot—Newfs are almost always peaceful and quiet in the car.

Although some Newfs are more laid-back than others, in the car as elsewhere, I have heard of few that ever jumped around or otherwise misbehaved in a moving vehicle. (What a disaster if they did!) Nor have I known a Newfie that suffered from car-sickness. The breed is famous for its history as a seafaring group, many of them, according to accounts in the literature, spending most of their lives on board ship, so perhaps they do have some inherent ability to cope well with motion. And perhaps they all think they are forever enroute "down to the sea again."

They can smell water, no doubt about that. And those that love the water—which are almost all—exhibit signs of excitement when they get a sniff of the stuff. Saltwater seems to please them the most, or maybe it just has a more powerful odor. Kasam, the only Newfoundland we ever owned that did not care to swim, responded the least to the tang of sea air. She would lift her head and give a few interested twitches of her nose as we neared a shore, but that was about it. Samantha expressed enormous interest in the proximity of any water—we swore she reacted to back-yard swimming pools and full ditches—and went wild at the smell of saltwater, her entire frame wriggling in synchronization with her nose, while her tongue darted in and out, savoring the taste of the air.

Water is a constant in Shauna's life. She is only inches from the deep water of our back-yard pond, along one side of which is strung the fence of her exercise yard, and scarcely farther than a Babe Ruth homer from the shore of Puget Sound. Yet, even she, when the wind blows across the Sound toward our house, heads for the deck or terrace. There she sits as tall as she can stretch, nose pointing straight upward, sucking in huge draughts of the salt-laden air. At such times, a look of particular bliss suffuses her whole being.

Newfies may hope that every trip will end at the seashore, but they happily accommodate themselves to any conditions or destination as long as they can *go*. Discomforts that drive the human occupants of the vehicle up the walls are stoically endured by all the Newfoundlands we have traveled with. One harrowing trip could have cost Samantha her life, yet she never once complained. She was our first Newfie, and we had absolutely no experience with taking dogs in the car. (Our former pet, a sweet little mixed-breed female named Ginger, got carsick in approximately two blocks, so was never taken anywhere except to the veterinarian.) We had done very little traveling ourselves and were totally unprepared for what occurred.

It was July and we were bound for Cape Cod—on a weekend! Our car had no air-conditioning, and we were all uncomfortable with the heat but surviving with the aid of open windows and the breeze created by the car's motion. Until we hit the approach to the bridge that leads to the Cape. Just south of Plymouth at 3 P.M., we found ourselves locked in a monstrous traffic jam. Miles of cars sat bumper to bumper, immobile in the blazing sun. So many vehicles were overheating and stalling that, even when the chance to inch ahead developed, the disabled cars created new bottlenecks. Wiser drivers shut off their engines and sat.

Everyone suffered. The most hale and vigorous youths wilted quickly; children, babies, elderly people, anyone in poor health— and Newfoundland dogs—were at real risk. Some people stepped out of their cars, but, with no shade anywhere, relief was not to be found that way.

Perhaps our own human misery was alleviated slightly by the concern we soon shared for Samantha: her distress was rapidly becoming acute. Her heavy coat of black fur was soaking up the midsummer heat like a sponge. Her increasingly labored panting was but a feeble weapon in the battle and served mainly to hasten dehydration. Unthinkable as it is to me now, we had taken no container of water. The only thing we had was a cooler—we always carried a few snacks with us including milk and fruit juice for the children, soft drinks and beer for us. Early that morning, we had dumped ice cubes around the cans and bottles and plastic containers in the cooler.

By the time we opened the cooler in the midst of that devilish ordeal only a few stray nubbins of ice remained, but the cans of liquid were quite cold and the water at the bottom was cool. We hauled out all the drinks and food containers and gave the children and ourselves juices to drink. Wiping off the drips of the juice cans on a towel had given me the idea to wet the towel and put it over Samantha's back—a good procedure, by the way, for helping dark-coated dogs cope with sun and heat. But it seemed most critical to first get some liquid *inside* her, so we pointed her nose into the cooler and told her to drink. But, what had seemed like an awful lot of ice cubes had melted down into only a bare inch or so of water in the bottom, and she drank up most of it in one take. A few moments later, we were tipping the cooler and she was licking up the last drops in the corner. Nothing left to wet the towel!

Wrong! We told Sammy to lie down, we spread the towel over her back and, can-by-can, we poured the chilled Cokes and then the cold beer over the towel. At first, the towel almost literally steamed. And what a stench—the warmed mixture of cola and beer was awesome! We knew we were breaking the law just to have opened containers of alcoholic beverages in the car, and we wondered if we would *ever* get out of jail, should a policeman stop us when we finally got under way again. One whiff of the interior of that car and I expect they would have thrown away all keys.

We did make it, at the end of what seemed like one of the longest days of our lives. Everyone survived. Our weekend was not quite as planned—most of it was spent trying to get the stickiness of the cokes and the smell of the beer out of Samantha's coat and the inside of the car.

We have never taken an automobile trip again without a large container of water and a cooler jammed as full as it can be with ice.

Years later and across more than the width of the continent, that precaution helped keep us and our beloved Kasam alive as we sat one summer Sunday in a line of cars on Orcas in the San Juan Islands of Washington State, during a seven-and-one-half-hour wait for a ferry back to Anacortes and home. We all drank water and some of the melted ice and draped both 'Sammy and our own heads with towels dipped in it. That time 'Sammy and I also found some shade during part of the afternoon in the ditch on the side of the car away from the sun, which helped.

No serious traffic jams blocked our late-summer trek with Becky from New York to Wisconsin the year we took Deborah off to college in Madison—just seemingly eternal hours covering seemingly endless miles of baked earth and smoldering cement across the prairies. The station wagon in which we took that trip was supposedly air-conditioned, but little of the cool made it all the way back to Becky in the rear. The poor thing had a good deal more than heat to contend with on that journey too.

It is amazing what a collection of materials constitute the essentials for one seventeen-year old college student. When I went away from home to enter the halls of higher learning, I had to go by train. One old steamer trunk from our attic was filled with bulky clothing such as boots, winter coat, and assorted other coverings designed to help endure winters that could, and twice *did* during my stay, touch down at forty below zero. The trunk also held a study lamp (we had to supply our own), a meager selection of books (my dictionary and two collections of poems), one or two framed photographs, and a very few, very special, trinkets. The trunk was sent by railway express. A large carton containing pillow, blankets, sheets, towels, and an old pair of draperies (we had to provide everything for our rooms except furniture and mattress— even throw rugs for the bare floor, but I did without those rather than ship more containers) was sent with the trunk. I took two largish and one small suitcase with me on the train.

Times had changed, however, and Deborah was going to be housed in a dormitory that was a palace compared to mine, so I thought there would be less to take. True, she did own more clothes than I ever had—and Wisconsin winters can be almost as harsh as Iowa's, so warm clothing is essential—and special comforts, such as "hot pots" for making tea or coffee or instant soup, were allowed (as they most emphatically were *not* in my day and place), but I had also neglected to consider how impossible it was for young people of my daughter's day to survive without records and record players. And hair dryers. And mammoth rollers for shaping the coiffures. And tennis racquets. And books. And at least one thousand other "basic necessities."

So we packed up cartons and tote bags and orange crates and suitcases. And more cartons and wall decorations and throw pillows. And more cartons. As the pile of things to go began to accumulate, I began thinking in terms of U-Hauls. We had, however, one of the huge station wagons that were common in the late '60s, and I am especially good at organizing space, so we thought we were okay. We were taking Becky, just for fun. She was really

Deb's dog and Deb thought it would be easier to part with her pet *there*, after getting launched into new quarters and a new life. Then, too, Becky would keep Don and me company on what we correctly surmised would be a slightly sad and lonely return trip.

To meet the challenge of getting all the "I-have-to-take-this-alongs" into the car and leave space for three people and a New-foundland, I took dozens of measurements of the vehicle's interior—cars are not boxes at all, they have curves and slopes and bumps in the darndest places—and made diagrams of the available spaces. Then I set to work with paper and pencil. Included in my list of measurements were Becky's dimensions, standing and lying down. I noted the space required for the latter two ways—flat on her side with legs extended, and upright on the chest ("sternal recumbency" in technical parlance) with legs tucked in close to the body. It crossed my mind that she could lie on top of a layer of other goods at least ten to twelve inches thick (in either position) but that plan was abandoned when I realized that if she couldn't stand up inside, there would be no way for her to enter or exit.

I settled for building a stall along one side of the rear compartment. The space reserved for her was the full height of the vehicle's interior back there, so she could stand and turn enough to reverse her weight from one hip to the other in the sternal position, but there was not room for her to lie on her side and stretch out her legs. I seem to remember the slot was fourteen inches wide, but I am not positive about that. She could not turn around, so the allotted area had to extend from the tailgate to the back of the back seat—that way she could get in the car from the rear and get out via the back seat and the side door.

The stall was formed by a row of orange crates and a mini-chest of drawers (packed full, of course) down the center of the rear compartment from front to back. They were wedged tightly into the tallest part of the area so they could not slide or topple onto Becky. To maximize driver visibility, Becky's stall was on the right side. (When she was lying down one could see out the right rear, adding to the view in the right mirror.) The entire left side of the rear compartment and of the back seat was filled to the ceiling. A space—not too different from Becky's stall and directly in front of it—remained on the right of the rear seat for one human passenger!

Every available inch was crammed. Soft things were stuffed into all the odd nooks and crannies. Space near human feet (except the driver's!) held small bags with overnight necessities for people and dog en route. The cooler with its cargo of ice and water had pride of place next to the person on the back seat. It was on top of other items and had a soft bag squeezed between it and the car roof so the whole pile would stay in place. Gaining access to the cooler's contents was a juggling act but, with the cooperation of the passenger in front, could be done without stopping the car.

Incredibly, it was a fun trip! Except for Deb's bout with asthma, an ailment she had outgrown years earlier but which reappeared as if disclaiming her readiness to leave childhood behind, we had a ball. We stopped at motels two nights along the way. Becky was taken for brisk runs each morning and evening (as well as once during the day at a roadside stop or near a restaurant); she was fed night and morning; she was combed and brushed briefly once a day; she was petted and loved and praised; she slept all night in air-conditioned coolness with legs stretched as far as they would go; and she was given cool water to drink anytime at all! She made a great hit with the arriving students as we unloaded Deb's belongings and helped her get settled, and even won the housemother's approval to walk the corridors and visit in the rooms. Deb told us she later met dozens of other students because of Becky; for weeks afterward, they would come up to her and ask about or comment on the dog they saw with her on that day. Some of those initial conversations blossomed into lasting friendships.

The trip home was strange. With the entire back empty and the rear seat folded down, the tailgate looked a mile away from where Don and I sat. Our one small suitcase and Becky's tote bag (food, dish, plastic bags for clean-up, grooming tools) were tucked in under the platform just behind the front seat, leaving what appeared to be an acre or more for Becky and the cooler. She had plenty of room to get up and down, to turn, to sprawl here, there, and yonder in every position possible. Did she? No. She tucked herself up against the back of our seat and moved scarcely less often or in a wider area than she had been able to on the outbound leg of the journey. It was as though she said, "Look, there's plenty of room, we don't need to leave Deb and her stuff back there. I can manage just fine in a tiny stall."

No other trip we took required a dog to be stowed in like inanimate cargo the way that one did, but several involved a collection of dogs confined closely together in the car and, all too often, they and we were packed together like sardines in motel rooms. Once, things got almost beyond the limit when we had *five* people and two Newfoundlands in one modest-sized accommodation. The room would have been tight but okay for the planned four of us and the dogs. At the last minute a friend of Deborah's joined us.

Candy had been living with us for a couple of months, but we had expected her to be back with her mother before the dog show in New Jersey for which both Becky and Shalom were entered and a room at a motel reserved. When the weekend arrived, Candy was still with us, so we squeezed all seven bodies and minimum luggage into the car. It was a big show, attracting so many exhibitors that we were informed on arrival there were no extra rooms. The best they could do was wheel in a cot. Along with the two double beds, scarcely any floor room was left for Newfoundlands and no space at all to groom them for the show except by picking up the cot and setting it atop one of the beds. We managed that—what we almost didn't manage was sharing one bathroom among five people, four of them female and two teen-age!

The bathroom played a major role in another dog/motel room escapade, this time for a different reason and one that was unusual in those days. Whether it is a question of regional differences or whether times have changed, I do not know, but in our travels with dogs in the Northeast, doors were rarely closed to pets. From cheap down-at-the-heels motels to Holiday Inns and others of their ilk and even high-priced New York City hotels, we were told only twice in all the years of dog-show and vacation trips that pets were disallowed. (Both times, by the way, were in less than high-quality establishments.) Indeed, various dogs of ours have been graciously accommodated—and have graced the hallways, rooms, lounges, and elevators—in some quite glamorous resorts and sophisticated urban hotels.

We have discovered the same attitudes do not prevail in the part of the world where we now live. It annoys us—and makes us *non*-customers of places we would otherwise be pleased to patronize. I do not like to be prejudged, negatively, which is what I think is happening when "no pets are allowed" signs go up. Our dogs have never done one whit of damage to people or property, and they would not travel with us if there was a chance they would. We would be more than willing to pay a deposit as security against such an eventuality and as a reassurance to those who do not know us or our pets.

One awful night in Vermont, however, we found ourselves in no position to take chances. On our way from somewhere to some-where else we had already run into several delays when a terrible summer storm hit. It got as dark as if a lid had been clamped on top of the world, and within a few minutes, we seemed verily to be inside a boiling pot. Sheets of rain swept in all directions, frothing on the windshield and running in foaming streams down the side windows, and churned across the roadway. The wind bellowed as it tossed shrubs, tree branches, every kind of debris, every which way. Jagged forks of lightening seemed to be aimed directly at us. I thought perhaps the devil had decided to stew us up for dinner and was trying to test us for doneness.

Even before the storm struck, we realized our intended destina-tion was no longer feasible. By the time the onslaught eased a bit, evening was rapidly approaching, so we decided to stop for the night in the next town. Apparently the weather had sent others scurrying early for cover because one-and-one-half hours later we had to accept the fact there was not a room for hire that night in that town. All of us—two children, two Newfoundland dogs, and two adults who felt they had already been through a wringer—needed bathroom facilities, needed to moisten parched throats, needed food, needed some comfort and rest.

There was nothing to do but drive on another half hour to the next dot on the map. That was Bennington, an even-smaller community than the last, but a college town, with more establishments of the kind we sought. With more visitors too, as it turned out, for something interesting seems always to be going on in a community dominated by an institution of Bennington's sort. Once again, we made the dreary rounds. By now, the rain had settled to a steady downpour that for all its greater calmness was no less wet, so Don's back-and-forthing from car to motel offices added the bonus of soggy clothes to his list of miseries.

At the far edge of town, we stopped at the only other place on our list (also full to the last room). Don probably looked pitiful and readily admits to trying to sound that way as he told the proprietor his story of hungry children and exhausted parents, and they agreed to make some telephone calls on our behalf. Jubilant, he returned to the car with the news that some eight or ten miles back the other way, a short way off the road we had taken into town, was a place with a room that was being saved for us. We went. We crossed fingers, legs, and even our eyes in an effort to ensure that no other bedraggled sojourners would grab our refuge first.

As we pulled into the driveway of Gray's (Inn? Motel?)—I will never forget "Gray's" in any case—I asked if he had mentioned pets. "No," he said and without another word parked well away from the office entrance. If those inside wondered why he chose to walk so far through the rain instead of pulling up near the door, they didn't say. They *did* say, "Yes, sir, we have the one room. We saved it. It is rather small but there are two beds. Actually, we didn't rent it earlier because we are planning to start work at that end of the building first thing in the morning and it will be noisy."

"It's fine, it's fine, it's fine," my husband said he kept assuring them. And, then—once an honest man, always an honest man (or almost anyway!)—he heard himself asking "Do you take dogs?"

The lady in charge, he says, looked quickly at him with "No" written all over her face, but said, instead, "I guess it's all right—he doesn't get on the bed, does he?" Don replied with utter truth, "Absolutely not." (There was not a "he," of course, rather *two* of them, both "shes," but in all honesty, none of our dogs has ever been allowed on a bed.) He told us he had a hard time, even in the condition he was in, not to smile at the thought of our two Newfs sharing two ordinary double beds with the four of us.

Just as he left the office, the lady called to say she would send towels down shortly, as the room had not been fully prepared. He failed to report that fact until we were in the room and milling around in an effort to distribute the six of us in the available spots and get ourselves organized. When a tap came at the door and the lady called out her errand, I panicked at the thought she might kick us out if she saw the dogs. So she stood waiting outside the door while Deb and I shoved and pulled and dragged two confused, hungry, weary Newfoundlands into the tiny bathroom. Deb had to push Becky into the tub and climb up on the toilet herself to make room for Samantha. I slammed the door on all three while Don admitted the lady with the towels.

Poor woman. She wanted to check the bathroom to make sure it had been cleaned. The three of us answered in unison, "No, no," "It's fine, it's clean," and "My sister is in there." She glanced around—no doubt observing that, indeed there were only three, not four, people in the room and, we were deathly afraid, probably about to inquire about the dog.

We literally removed the towels from her hands and bade her a hearty good night as she backed reluctantly through the still-open door. It was too dark for anyone to see anything that night but next morning, Don walked one dog at a time, hoping that if he was observed, one would look so like the other, it would be assumed there was only one. By then, of course, we had had our desperately needed rest and food and showers and were ready to leave anyway.

My husband simply did not want anyone to think he had seemed to tell a lie, by omission at least.

I did put a little thank-you note on the bureau before we left, expressing our gratitude for the hospitality they had extended to "the Jagers," but without enumerating the members of the family.

The Cat's Pajamas

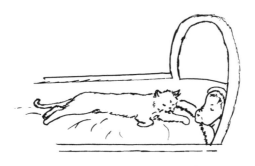

Kindness to animals has always been an honored precept in our family. We have never allowed ourselves or our children to exploit pets. Well—almost never. I must confess to one interlude with one animal—a cat named Henrietta—when we slid dangerously close to the edge, if not over it. Yet I did not then and do not now, quite feel that what we did was wrong. The simple reason, I guess, is that the cat seemed actually to enjoy her role in spite of the discomfort it may have entailed.

When our first child, Deborah, was only a few weeks old, I began putting her outdoors in her buggy whenever there was the soft air and sunshine that April now and then provides. The outings were at her nap time, or, rather, her hoped-for nap time, for Deb was not a sleeper. (Not at any rate, until she was old enough to go to school and *had* to get up.) In order to get even minimal housework done, I often had to simply put her down and let her cry. The backyard was a safe place—small town, last house on the street, fenced yard, earlier era!—and that slight distance made the crying a bit less harrowing to me.

It quickly became apparent that the alfresco ambience must really have been beneficial, because, after only a short time outdoors, she usually stopped crying and actually slept. It was a miracle. I was too grateful for the beautiful silence and peace to risk disrupting it by going to check. Someone once said that nothing is more certain to wake a sleeping baby than the sound of a mother's head hitting a pillow, and I had certainly learned that Deb's snoozes were so light that even breathing nearby could trigger her wake-up bell.

Our breathing. But apparently not Henrietta's. Nor her purr, which, I might add, was a mighty rumble. That cat's motor mouth could wake anyone. Yet it turned out that Henrietta and her purring were the undercover elements of Deb's outdoor naps. By glancing out at the parked buggy now and then, it was not long before I discovered the secret. Within moments after I walked away from the screaming babe, a furry white feline body slipped up and over the side of the buggy and disappeared within. Almost instantly the screams stopped, the crying tapered off, the baby slept. The cat, after awhile, slipped out of the buggy and away.

Henrietta had *never* done that indoors—in bassinet or buggy. But, from the day Deb and I came home from the hospital, she had paced and meowed and appeared distraught whenever the infant cried. Perhaps she knew she could handle it if I'd only let her, but sensed that I would not knowingly have tolerated such interference. Outdoors, she got her chance. And created a role she would not relinquish for more than two years.

Never before or since have I yearned as fervently for a mild, dry spring, for the only days of semipeace that I had were when Henrietta played nursemaid in the yard. And then, one cold and rainy day, it dawned on me that what worked outside might well be put to use indoors. As I laid the squalling infant down for the umpteenth time, I yielded to temptation: I plucked the pacing Henrietta from the floor, and dumped her in the bassinet. In an instant she was stretched on top of the blanket, tight along the side of the crying baby, face-to-face with her, purring up a storm. Even the batterings of the tiny flailing arms and fists did not make Henrietta flinch. Peace reigned within minutes.

Friends warned me of the health hazard I courted. A neighbor even told me that cats *kill* babies by "stealing their breath." Well—it was probably an unsanitary practice at best, but the risk seemed a good trade for the incessant crying that presented a serious threat to *my* mental health if not to the infant's well-being.

Once or twice we tried to substitute Jo-Jo, Henrietta's litter mate, who had always displayed less independence and was far and away the more biddable of the two creatures in other situations, but she fled from the restless, noisy baby as if chased by the devil—a response I often shared with her, in thought if not in deed.

Soon, at naptimes and bedtimes, scouting the house for Henrietta became as much a part of the ritual as changing diapers and tucking blankets. Henrietta's independence had formerly taken her out of the house and away for hours at a time, occasionally for entire days, but, curiously, we rarely had to hunt far when bedding the babe.

By the time Deborah could talk (and it's not too surprising that her first word was neither "Ma-ma" or "Da-da" but Kit-tee"), she would start demanding Henrietta as soon as bedtime preparations began. As she grew from babe to toddler, "Hemmy! Hemmy, come!!" would be her imperious demand.

By then, randomly flailing fists were the least of "Hemmy's" miseries. Small arms would grasp and clutch at fur, pull and squeeze, and sometimes threaten to smother the poor creature. We did try to see that the cat was not choked or crushed, but she seemed to have the ability to wriggle loose from real strangleholds and the willingness to endure a lot. Once the child was fast asleep, a sleek white body would glide down the stairs and usually head for the door and out. Then we knew our child was peacefully slumbering.

Now and again we were struck with fear: What if something happened to Henrietta—if she sickened or died? Would Deborah ever sleep again? She loved her stuffed toys, and played and slept with many—but never *instead* of her Henrietta. One of the few times we could not find the cat at Deborah's bedtime became a two-hour nightmare as the shrieks and demands for "Hemmy" grew and persisted while Don searched house and yard and several acres of our part of town for the errant nursemaid. When Henrietta was found—stalking mice at sunset in a nearby field—she meekly gave up the game and returned to her responsibility.

None of us can remember when or how Deb finally learned to sleep without the cat—but little by little the need shrank, and the demands became fewer, so that sometime after Deborah's second birthday, Henrietta was able to shed the shackles she had so graciously donned.

Did she enjoy her release, or did she long to be needed as before? We can't know. We only know that before another year had passed, Henrietta was gone. We never knew where or, for sure, when. For weeks we looked, called, advertised in newspaper and on radio, offered a reward (and answered many a call about "stray" white cats), and checked routinely with shelters and other agencies. No trace of her, dead or alive, was ever found. Her littermate, Jo-Jo, lived to be seventeen, dying the year Deborah was a senior in high school.

A Fence Is for What?

"It doesn't need to be tight to the ground everywhere," I said to the man who had agreed to fence in the back half of the two-acre plot on which our new house was going up. "Just string the wire between trees where you can and put posts where you have to. The idea is simply to remind the dogs where the edge of their space is so they don't absent-mindedly wander off." To make my point even stronger, I added, "Our Newfoundlands don't want to go anywhere else—we don't need to *enclose* them."

Clearly, the idea didn't sit well with this fellow—a retired farmer who loved fences and took pride in building them straight and strong and nestled so firmly to the earth that ants had trouble crawling under. Our piece of land was rough, rocky, pitted and humped, and heavily overgrown with trees and shrubs. There was even a forty-foot-or-so stretch of an ancient, crumbling stone wall along one part of the rear border that I had suggested might serve as sufficient barrier there. He had absolutely balked at that and won his point by adding that it would be more costly to do so—the heaps of fallen stones at both ends of the standing section would have to be cleared in order to set posts for stopping and restarting the wire fence.

And money was very much the name of the game at that moment. What had seemed to us like a sensibly generous budget for our building and moving-in costs had shrunk, as all such budgets seem inevitably to do, faster and farther than we could believe. We were definitely at the compromise stage with the remaining elements, so I prevailed in my insistence to cut costs every possible way on the fences. In addition to reducing labor by asking the poor man to do a lesser job than he wished, I also changed the specs for the main-yard fencing, back in the trees and brush, to ordinary sheep wire—only five feet high, with mesh about five-by-seven inches—rather than the seven-foot, one-by-two-inch mesh we had originally planned.

Certain parts of the original fencing plan would not be shortchanged. We decided not to compromise on the face we showed the world. Handsome redwood boards, lined with wire, were used at the fronts to blend with and not destroy the beauty of our lovely glass-and-cedar house. An ultra-secure small pen for bitches in heat was essential—to keep them *in* and uninvited male suitors *out.* With a small revision, we now decided it could serve double duty as a puppy pen. Our breeding plans were modest. We meant to have only one actively producing female at a time and expected to have only about one litter a year, so a combined-use pen appeared feasible. We could add another one later if it was ever needed. We also decided to postpone partitioning off a smallish piece of the main fenced area as a second general-purpose pen. It would be useful, but it, too, could be done later. Plans for the kennel part of the daylight basement were also pared down from the original. One small room connecting with the security pen was made bitch-in-heat- and puppy-safe, while the rest of the area, leading to the main yard, was left open and relatively unfinished.

We were newcomers to the dog-breeding world. Actually, we were still newcomers to the Newfoundland-dog world. Until we moved into that house, we had lived with only three adult Newfies—and had had one litter. All had been utterly content to be homebodies, never wanting to be far from their people's sides, let alone beyond the small fenced yard at the house. Like most novices we had not yet found out how much we had to learn. 'Sicha was about to enter the scene and correct some of our misconceptions.

But, even before 'Sicha, (who was one of the first litter born at our new place) grew up to drive us all crazy with her wanderlust, we discovered that fences are two-way things: while "casual" ones may keep in creatures that have no desire to get out, they do little to keep out others that want in.

It was the beginning of summer when we moved—an exceptionally hot and humid one, even for upstate New York. Because the dog-room floors were concrete, the Newfies were happiest sprawled there, and I took to leaving the main door open nights as well as days, so they could come and go freely between the indoors and the large pen. Obviously other creatures found the cool of the basement attractive too: nearly every morning I found anywhere from one to half-a-dozen moles, field mice, and chipmunks in the dog room—sometimes alive and frisky on or behind shelves, stacks of dog-food cases, or the grooming table, and sometimes quite dead, probably after too-rough handling by playful Newfs. The uninvited guests worried me because of their potential to carry disease and parasites, but still I resisted shutting the dogs in all night, and I certainly didn't want to close them out, away from the interior coolness. Besides, I reasoned, they were near all those other creatures other times when they were outdoors anyway.

Nevertheless, it was a jolt when I entered the dog room one morning to find one extra *canine* creature curled up asleep next to one of the Newfs. The newcomer was a cute little beagle-sized mix of some sort—no collar or other identification—friendly as could be and so thin it was probably attracted even more by the possibility of food than by the coolness. The Newfs had clearly adopted it without a second thought and acted as though they quite approved when I prepared an extra bowl of breakfast for the guest. We considered letting it join the family permanently, but first I called the local animal shelter to check on reports of lost pets in case its owner was searching for it. While I waited for a response, the visitor vanished—

exiting, no doubt, as it had come, through any of dozens of spaces under the fence that were adequate for such a small body.

We never saw that one again, but other—less amenable—visitors arrived. Very early one morning, a wild ruckus from below took me downstairs at the nearest thing to a run I could manage when startled from sleep. There, high atop a stack of fifty-pound bags of dog food crouched a hissing, snarling tom cat of no small dimensions. The Newfs were leaping and lunging in a downright angry manner (an unusual sight indeed) and barking up a chorus of cacophonous proportions that must have assaulted the eardrums of everyone within a square mile. Blood splashed and splattered from one Newfie nose where a cat claw had connected. The results looked more alarming than they proved to be on later examination, but that event must have come as quite a shock to all the dogs, accustomed as they were to living in peace and mutual respect with our cats. I do believe they had decided that visitor needed to have some manners drummed into it.

When we finally were able to corral the dogs in the other part of the downstairs (much against their better judgment—I'm sure they did not think it safe to let me go unprotected into the room with that feline beast), the cat, seeing its chance, took off like a streak. How or why it had ever ventured into that arena baffles me; I suspect it may have asked itself the same question.

By that time, a litter of puppies was already scampering all over the puppy-room and pen—possibly a contributing factor in the Newfies' response to the belligerent cat's visit—and Holly had been told she could choose one female to keep. It would be her own dog to train and, later, to show, but it would be used as breeding stock also, assuming it turned out to be of adequate quality. Years later, we had many a laugh about 'Sicha's "breeding quality," which was prodigious, but did us no good, and about her showability, which Holly would have enjoyed, but which was nil. At the time Holly made her choice, it appeared a sensible one, and the little girl was dubbed "Ganshalom's Nesicha Shomeret," the name being more or less the Hebrew equivalent of "Ganshalom's Guardian Princess."

One might assume that guardianship entails remaining near the persons, objects, or areas to be guarded, but perhaps our Hebrew was so botched (as we were informed on occasion by Hebrew scholars) that 'Sicha didn't understand what her name implied in the way of duty. For she became a chronic runaway.

First, she became a *runt*. No indication was apparent in her early months that she would simply stop growing too soon. She developed, in fact, in a classically perfect way—beautifully proportioned, balanced, lithe, strong, healthy, and altogether quite promising. By the age of nine or ten months, however, she began to look definitely undersized alongside other Newfs of her age. She was also extraordinarily swift and much more finely coordinated than her more lumbering colleagues. She amazed us with her hunting feats, catching all manner of running and leaping wild creatures. The catch was the thing with her, and since she had the traditional soft mouth of a retriever plus the kindly disposition of a Newf, most of her quarry were released unharmed—except for the fright they surely must have suffered.

One day we watched her go after a large pheasant, laughing at her foolishness in attempting such a hopeless goal—the bird simply took to flight each time 'Sicha got almost within striking distance. She didn't give up, though, and there must have been some especially tasty morsels in the weeds and grasses of the fenced area, for the pheasant disdained the safety of the meadow beyond and stayed inside the dog yard—one time too often. As we watched in disbelief, 'Sicha's patience and swiftness paid off, and the pheasant's take-off was cut short as it found itself flapping wildly, wings full-spread, securely held inside a Newfie's jaws.

Holly, horrified, ran out into the pen—and 'Sicha, of course, ran straight to her with her prize. Holly grabbed 'Sicha's collar, dodged the furiously beating wings, and cried "Give!" 'Sicha, always the obedient child (when she was within earshot of her mistress), *gave*. The jaws parted, and the—probably considerably older and, one hopes, much wiser—pheasant flew to freedom, intact save for a feather or two.

Holly had given extra attention to obedience and show training during those months while she waited for 'Sicha to grow large and solid and impressive enough to do some conformation winning and earn points toward a championship. The wait was in vain—'Sicha remained undersized all her life and never earned a point in shows. Along the way, though, it occurred to us that if we could just keep her from running all her calories away, she still *might* grow. For 'Sicha had developed a taste for travel.

All Newfies like to go in cars with their people. That was okay with 'Sicha too, but it wasn't enough. The first time she discovered a low spot in the ground, where she could slip under the fence, and went exploring, we didn't know she was gone until she came trotting up the driveway, panting and full of burrs, and begged to get *in* the pen for water and a rest. Don found the spot where she had gone out—he thought—and plugged it with stones. He plugged a couple of others for good measure.

The next day, she simply found another and took off. He plugged it, and she found another. It was not long before we were quite weary of the game. But 'Sicha was not. We would confine her for days to the security of the puppy pen, while all of us hauled rocks, pounded metal stakes into the fence at ground level, dragged heavy logs and wired them to the bottom of the fence, dug and piled earth against boards and stones, and did our best to fence her in.

Each time she was released from the puppy pen—naturally more ravenous than ever for exercise—she would find a new place, or dig out an old one, and go for a run through the countryside. Once, when she couldn't find a way under the fence—or perhaps she was bored with that procedure—we saw her leap halfway up and climb the rest like a ladder. Another time she went *through* by forcing her head into one of the spaces and pushing until a joint came apart and the wires spread enough for her to slide through. She left a lot of hair behind, but that didn't even slow her down. Sometimes, driving home from work or errands, one of us would discover her trotting alongside a busy road, just inches from speeding wheels. We would stop and open the car door, and she would hop in, delighted to see us and quite pleased to have a ride home—blissfully unconcerned with our worry and distress.

In those days, a young man who was a student at Cornell sometimes did yard work for us, so, worn out with the effort ourselves, we assigned him the task of 'Sicha-proofing the dog yard. Armed with wheelbarrow, wire, shovel, and a strong back, he undertook to make the pen into a fortress. Day after day, after classes until dark, on Saturdays, and many Sundays, Jim matched wits with a ninety-pound dog. After he used all the stones from the old stone fence, we bought cinder blocks. After he used all the logs from fallen trees, we had other dead and dying ones cut down to add to the supply. We paid him for many hours of work. And many more. And many, many more. (Perhaps 'Sicha wanted to help him work his way through Cornell?)

Several times, Jim won the battle. For a week or two, 'Sicha would seem to have been bested. We would sigh with relief, close our thinning check book, and trot out a laugh or two about the whole thing. And about then, a neighbor would call and report that two of our dogs had just romped through their yard. For, by that time, Shalom was going too. Shalom was our huge male—at one hundred eighty pounds, he was exactly twice 'Sicha's size—very valuable, very unsuitable for endurance runs, very stupid about cars, very lazy, very content to stay home—and utterly devoted to 'Sicha. The last thing Shalom wanted to do was to roam the countryside, but ever since his "little girl" had come of age and had her first heat (during which she had, of course, been confined to the security pen), he had gone berserk whenever she slipped through a hole and took flight.

Shalom could not get his massive head, much less his whole bulk, through the places 'Sicha used as exits, but he had something else going for him—power. We began to find entire sections of fence bent back and up from the bottom, sometimes ripped loose from posts, and, more than once, actually *split* from the bottom up. We surmised (correctly, as we discovered later when we witnessed one event) that she made a space big enough to scrape through (by digging and pushing and pulling with teeth and claws) which gave him enough room to push his head under and then use his enormous neck and shoulders to rip open the wire. Twice he had slashes on his sides from the ends of broken fencing.

One day, Jim himself drove up with both the prodigals in his car—Shalom so exhausted he all but fell out when the door was opened—and told us he had found the two on campus, miles away! When he spied them, 'Sicha had been flitting back and forth on one of the main quadrangles, absolutely delighted with all the people and activity there, while Shalom struggled, pitifully weary, to keep her in his sights. Once more, Jim hauled out the tools and set to work to patch the latest breach of the rampart walls. But it was clear to all of us that the game had run its course. 'Sicha had lost a few battles, but she had won the war.

Our friends, the Linns, who owned Edenglen Kennels, were not dismayed by the challenge. They had, after all, more than fifty acres at the end of a half-mile of private road. They had streams and lake frontage to add swimming to the possibilities for exercise that 'Sicha seemed to require. And they would be able to breed her—we could handle only one producing bitch at a time and 'Sicha's mother, Becky, was still it. Motherhood seemed a promising way to help settle her down and keep her home.

It worked. We all lived happily—for many years, if not ever after. 'Sicha produced dozens of beautiful puppies for them and made a name for herself on the international scene. We took, in exchange, a sweet, quiet, lovely young bitch we named Shir Hashirim (Song of Songs) who later gave us a litter that included my precious Kasam.

Oh, it's true—'Sicha did pull a few runaways on the Linns between litters, and even got all the way to the main highway on several occasions. Worse—she didn't go alone. Of all the dogs the Linns had, the one—the only one—they soon learned could not be let out at the same time, or both would vanish instantly, was Tucker. Their gorgeous, famous, award-winning stud dog. Tucker—'Sicha's father.

Red Light for Danger

BELIEVE!

Dogs, some people say, serve as sentinels of danger—acting strangely just before earthquakes, tornados, and other natural disasters. I have never read a scientific treatise on the theory, but there is no question in my mind that some dogs do attempt to alert their people to what the dogs perceive as dangers.

Our first Newfoundland, Samantha, was a worrier, a busybody, a nag. We often referred to her as "the policeman." She seemed to think everybody's business (other dogs' as well as people's) was her business and, furthermore, that most creatures, herself excluded, just didn't have good sense. She acted as though the burdens of the world were hers to bear, solo.

Although she loved the water, as is traditionally the case with Newfoundlands, she didn't think it was a safe or suitable milieu for *any* other creature—not other dogs, not even other Newfoundlands, and certainly not human beings. Indeed, she nearly drowned several people, including our daughter Holly, and at least one other Newfoundland, our Shalom, in the process of getting them *out* of the water—against their wishes.

Samantha also distrusted heights and became frantic with worry, barking herself hoarse, when people were on our roof to do needed repairs. Once, when a man climbed a tree to cut a dead limb, I thought she would lose her mind.

One evening, she drove all of us to distraction with her incessant efforts to make us see something wrong, somewhere to the west. She leapt and pawed at the fence forming the western boundary of the dog pens, barking, yelping, trying to dig under or climb over, and looking repeatedly, first toward us as we peered out windows, and then westward again.

We could see nothing unusual. Beyond the yard was the road. Across the road, more trees and shrubs, as the ground sloped downward toward the eastern lake shore a mile or more away. Another mile or so beyond was the opposite shore, and then the land lifted again into the long ridge known as West Hill.

We could perceive nothing that would explain her frantic behavior. We tried to soothe her, we ordered her to stop, we even dragged her indoors—to no avail. In or out, she would not stop her wild efforts to elicit some kind of action from us. Around midnight she gave up—possibly from utter exhaustion—and consented to come into the dog rooms and go to her blanket. We, gratefully, went to ours.

The lead item on the local news next morning was the story of a devastating fire at a huge poultry farm a good five or six miles away on West Hill. Thousands of chickens had perished as massive barns burned to the ground. The angle was such that we had not been able to see the flames, although in daylight we would certainly have seen the plume of smoke. Could she have seen flames? Her vantage point outdoors was considerably lower and even more screened by shrubbery than ours. Could she have smelled the smoke? Possibly, but the wind had not been right to make that feasible. Could she *hear* something—the crackling sounds of rampant fire, the voices of shouting people—so many miles away? There was little doubt in our mind that her senses had picked up something from the fire that spelled danger in her mind. She had put her heart and soul into trying to warn us.

A long time later—perhaps several years—she set up an almost identical uproar one winter evening, again looking to the west. After several fruitless attempts to quiet her, one of the girls quipped, "Maybe there's another fire on West Hill." There was. This one was smaller but closer, directly across the lake from us and not far above the shore. With little besides leafless winter trees in the way, we could see the leaping flames with clarity, and assumed that she could too. An unanswerable question arose, however, when we realized she had been frantically trying to warn us a *good half-hour* before we were able to see the fire.

We should not have been surprised on either occasion, for long before the two instances of fire, we had learned to "listen" carefully to Samantha's warnings. What she perceived as danger—another dog swimming competently in a pond, a safety-strapped professional trimming a tree—was not always a situation worthy of worry, but when she made her announcements there was always an explanation. And it was sometimes a valid warning.

Our first experience with Samantha's alarm instincts had been when she was scarcely six months old. Like most families, we had a well-established bedtime routine. Part of my final chores included putting Samantha out the back door for her last bathroom opportunity of the night and finishing up last-minute kitchen duties while she was out. Often there were pots and pans, left earlier to dry in the rack, to be put away; the coffee pot, left on "warm" with any remaining brewed beverage inside, had to be unplugged; and snack foods that might have been gotten out during the evening were to be stowed. Then I would open the back door to let Samantha in, close and lock it, and walk with her through the kitchen, turning off the light as I went. Together, we would go through the house and up the stairs. She would accompany me as I stepped into each child's bedroom to check on them and then retire to her place near our bed while I tended to my personal nighttime preparations.

On the evening in question, she and I got only to the landing of the stairs when she turned and went back down. I called, she paused and looked at me, but after a long, hesitant moment proceeded, not up, but to the back of the house. Assuming that she had failed to complete her outdoor chores the first time, I went back and let her out again. She went meekly enough but spun and came back in before I'd closed the door. Exasperated, I shoved her out. The door was barely closed before she scratched to come in.

Once again we traipsed up the stairs. Once again, she hesitated and stayed that time on the landing, while I made my rounds without her. Coaxing eventually got her to our bedroom, and a sharp command, "Lie down," was reluctantly obeyed. But not for long.

For an hour I did battle with her. Commands, reassurances, scoldings—each settled her for only a few minutes. Time after time, she went to the top of the stairs and, plainly as words could have done, "asked" me to go down with her. Time after time, deciding at last that she must have a digestive upset and therefore need to go out, I made the trip with her to the back door. Time after time, she balked at going out—but paced and whimpered at me, clearly upset.

On each trip through the kitchen I flipped on the light; on each trip back, I flipped it off. As I got into bed after each climb of the stairs, more and more weary, more and more distraught, I spoke with increasing sharpness and mounting anger. Eventually, in my frustration, I resorted to threats and slaps. She was obviously hurt and confused by my behavior, but undeterred.

Six times we had traced and retraced our paths. On the seventh trip, for some reason—exhaustion, hopelessness?—I did not even pause to turn on the kitchen light. Which is why I noticed it—the little red light on the coffee pot, indicating it was still plugged in.

Even then I perceived no relationship among the night's events but merely yanked out the plug, glad I'd noticed *that* and given some purpose to my endless ups and downs. The instant I did, Samantha turned and all but leapt up the stairs. By the time I got to the bedroom she was flopped in her usual place, as totally contented and peaceful as an animal could be. She looked at me—I swear with gratitude in her eyes and a smile on her face—and thumped her huge tail in satisfaction.

Within minutes, Samantha was sound asleep, snoring as usual, while I lay awake for a long, long time, wondering how she had known the coffee pot was plugged in—I presume she must have noticed the red light when we left the kitchen the very first time—but, more important, how could she have imagined that was something to worry about? We will never know, nor will we ever know how long she would have continued her demands in the face of my increasing displeasure, had I not at last heeded the red light of danger she worked so diligently to make me see.

Bronx Cheer

It was the best of weekends and the worst. It was a roller coaster of events that ranged from turmoil to triumph and was overloaded with pit-of-the-stomach sensations. In fact, there was considerable evidence that some of the digestive-tract involvement was more than symbolic.

The whole turbulent to-do revolved around a dog show. Just an ordinary dog show. Or so we thought. Had we known how bad it would be—ugly, uncomfortable setting, no trophies worth having, unfriendly ambience, miserable weather—we would have paid to stay away. Had we known how wonderful it would be, we would have crawled to it. The rest of the weekend fitted itself neatly into the same contradictory pattern.

Our second Newfoundland, Edenglen's Becky, had come to us full-grown, already named, already a mother, and exquisitely beautiful. We were never able to totally reconcile the cute-little-girlness of the name, Becky, with the regal image she projected. Her lovely face and form, her elegant bearing, dramatically dark and glossy coat, and utter grace of movement were only enhanced by the pure sweetness of her disposition and a kittenish playfulness that burst at times like a genie from a bottle. At one show, several years and litters later, when she had made a name for herself in the ring as a queenly performer, Deborah was running her with the others of her class around a ring at the show in Bucks County, Pennsylvania. The setting there is lovely, as is all of Bucks County, it was late spring, the weather was superb, and the rapidly moving animals, all groomed to the teeth, shone in the sun as they circled for the judge's and the spectators' perusal. Becky was literally floating over the grassy sward, head high, feathers wafting in the breeze—a poetic vision.

Suddenly there was chaos. Deb found herself almost spilled as she was pulled up short on the advance end of a lead, still firmly attached of course to the neck of a rolling, spinning, ecstatically wriggling ball of black fur, on her back in the grass some four or five feet behind. Becky had found that plush sweet grass irresistible. She had thrown herself down, all four feet and tail madly gyrating in the air, pink belly to the sun, utterly indifferent to ring etiquette and to the on-coming stream of handlers and their charges—who had to veer and lurch and leap to avoid the unexpected obstacle in their path.

It was over in moments. A tug of the lead, a command (tinged more than a wee bit with sharpness), and Becky righted herself. One or two brisk shakes, executed with an elegance not unlike a well-mannered lady giving a discreet pat or two to her coiffure, and she joined her ringmates with the greatest aplomb. Deborah's poise had not fared so well, and, whether it was Becky's romp or Deb's loss of cool, there was no blue ribbon for us that day.

No such temptations as soft grass and spring sunshine existed at the Bronx show on our earlier weekend. Neither that blighted section of the great metropolis nor the Armory in which the show was held bore any remote resemblance to rural, affluent Pennsylvania, and the weather compared as unfavorably as the surroundings. It was March. Steely-gray curtains of rain fell nonstop from a sky that looked more like a heavy iron lid than a heavenly dome and was swept in great sheets through the high wide-open end of the dismal structure. Concrete floors were grimy and slippery with oil, soot, and water. The banks of lights high in the enormous steel rafters overhead glared down but were hopelessly outmatched by the gloom. An icy chill permeated every corner of the cavernous building.

It was doubtful if anything could have done serious battle with the grimness, but no one seemed to have tried. There was not even the usual sparkle of silver and crystal trophies displayed on the tables—the prizes to be won at that show were ugly blue-and-yellow striped envelopes containing two, three, or five one-dollar bills, marked for distribution according to class and breed. A pile of ribbons in the usual hues (but without even rosettes attached as they generally are for major wins) provided the only color and warmth to be seen. But we already had such a hefty headstart on wretchedness that the dreary scene at the show seemed more appropriate than not. What we had eagerly looked forward to as an exciting few days of family fun had assumed the earmarks of a nightmare in the making.

We were bare beginners, utter novices, in the world of pure-bred dogs and shows. The four of us—Don and myself and Deborah and Holly, then sixteen and ten years old, had been to one real show and one match show. The "real" one was a Newfoundland Specialty (no other breeds participating) and everyone had been kind when I walked into the ring with Becky, so totally uninformed about what I was supposed to do that that is *all* I did—walked—in the ring with her. I didn't "stack her up" or even stand her as required, I didn't move her correctly, I just walked around and mostly stood like a lump, with her on the end of the lead. We should have died of embarrassment but were too ignorant of protocol to even do that.

Vaguely aware after that episode that we could use some help, we asked and were advised to enter a few match shows. Sanctioned matches are organized and run essentially like regular shows, except wins don't count toward earning championship points. One of their major purposes is to serve as training ground for beginning handlers or as practice for young dogs. Experienced handlers, we learned later, may put a novice dog through its paces at half-a-dozen such events before taking it into the full-fledged competition of a point show; beginning handlers may participate in dozens of matches as preliminaries to the real thing. Heaven only knows what sensible beginners with an untried animal would consider sufficient preparation.

Because my one excursion into the ring had made it clear I was not equal to the task, we decided to let Deb assume the handler's mantle. Becky was, in all but official ownership, her dog anyway—from the beginning of their acquaintance they had spoken a private language to each other that no one else could hear or understand—so Deborah and Becky were entered in the next match show held in our part of the world. And, true to our usual "fools-rush-in" approach, that was the only "practice" event either was ever to be in.

In all fairness, what ensued might have convinced anyone that such efforts were totally unnecessary. Those two babes-in-the-woods nearly walked off with the whole bundle at their one and only match. Becky won her class, thereby earning the right to compete for Best-of-Breed. When she and her young mistress walked off with that ribbon and trophy too, we were delighted, of course, but would have been more pleased (and surprised) had we realized how relatively seldom such an honor goes to bitches. (The males of most dog breeds, being generally larger and more dramatic, tend to hog the top ranks in a most ungentlemanly fashion.)

Having captured the Best-of-Breed designation, Becky was entitled to compete with the best of each of the other thirty-some working breeds in the Group showing. By that time we were proud but scarcely astonished as we stood and watched our two girls placed at the pinnacle of the Working Group. Ah, we had so much to learn! Achievements of that caliber, even in match shows, are rare (if ever) events in the lives of dog-show participants. It was unthinkable that a first-time handler and an unshown (except for one almost-showing) animal (and a bitch at that) could have taken a Group first.

The day was growing long, we were tired, people and dogs needed food—it is a minor miracle that we did not leave before the final event, that high moment in any show when the group winners compete for the headiest of all awards—Best in Show. It would have been a monumental gaffe to have departed before the six group winners, chosen from several hundred, were displayed and judged. Fortunately, curiosity kept us there. Becky did not win that award—few dogs ever reach the Best-in-Show pinnacle. Now, many years and many shows later, we understand that winning a Group first, even in a match show, is a coveted achievement. We wish we could recapture that glorious moment. It had all seemed too easy.

Rare as such early success is, it does demonstrate that a beautiful dog can go far in spite of greenhorn handling, especially if the person is endowed, as Deborah is, with a natural gift for relating to animals. As we discovered at the Bronx show.

Spurred by the easy match-show win, we decided to go for the points that lead to championship by entering regular shows. The Bronx show looked promising: it was at a good time for us, and Don's parents lived in Brooklyn so we could combine a family visit with the show. They, like most apartment dwellers, had no room for four of us—much less a Newfoundland dog—so I booked a room at a motel chosen solely for its proximity to the show site. What an unholy mistake that was! It was hideous.

When a friend of ours, a delightful woman with whom I worked, learned that we were going to the city for the weekend, she asked if she could ride along. She had errands there and friends in Manhattan where she could stay, and we thought her company could only add spice to our adventure so we readily agreed. Her charm and wit may have been our salvation, although her body (slight as it was) and her luggage (also minimal) did cause us to strain the seams and the shock absorbers of our small station wagon nearly to the breaking point. A 135-pound dog, luggage for five people, and canine food and equipment for three days and a show filled the back-back about as full as one adult and two well-grown children did the back seat. Two other adults, miscellaneous parcels, snacks, and handbags crammed the front.

The trip down was not bad, as seven-hour, everybody-squeezed-together-in-a-moving-vehicle trips go, although Deb was ominously quiet, no doubt already running the fever that would reach a high of nearly 103 before morning. The rain that saved itself to coincide with our arrival in the city—which also coincided with rush hour and the beginnings of hunger pangs—did little to help us find our way through the unfamiliar streets of New York's northern reaches. Never a garden spot at its best, the Bronx looked cheerless indeed in the waning light of a March evening through the splattered windows of the car. Every single unattractive element of that benighted borough was distilled in the squalid surroundings and depressing structure that constituted our motel. The only "grounds" were the filthy parking lot, decorated with piles of soggy garbage in every corner, potholes filled with foul black goo, and rain-drenched litter blowing wildly back and forth.

Inside it was drier but scarcely warmer or cleaner. We really were unsure whether sheets had been changed or not—their streaked grayish color could have covered a multitude of sins, the sorts of which we preferred not to dwell upon. Cracked plastic furniture, stained carpet, rust-streaked bathroom fixtures, dusty draperies, and an incredibly ugly conglomeration of colors completed the decor. Along with a metal space heater that we found would help take the edge off the chill when it was turned on but which extracted a price in noise and fumes. All night we turned it first on, in an attempt to stop shivering long enough to sleep, then off to be able to breathe and have a measure of quiet, then on again as the dampness and chill pervaded our bones. Our flips of the heater switch were mostly in conjunction with our efforts to cope with Deborah's mounting illness. It was a night to remember.

Among the room's many quaint features were its lack of a telephone, a fact we had discovered on arrival when our passenger, Bettye, came in to call her friends and arrange for Don to drop her somewhere to meet them. We, of course, also needed to call my in-laws to make arrangements for the following day. Don and Bettye had discovered that a pay phone was available in the office, but they were allowed to use it only grudgingly after being led past a ferocious-appearing German Shepherd, restrained with considerable effort by the man in the office. They were also informed that no one was admitted to the office under any circumstances after dark. If emergencies were to occur, apparently they should be planned for the daylight hours.

Bettye had taken one look at our quarters and, with a glance at our beautiful Becky said, "Well, this may be okay for you—but *I* don't think it's fit for a dog." She was right. Where was I to exercise our immaculate, groomed, gracious, and proper Becky-dog in the muck that surrounded us? We finally found a spot between an honest-to-goodness junk yard and an old shed, where she did her necessary business. Somehow she managed to imbue the undertaking with an aura of fastidiousness in spite of the piles of garbage and carpet of broken glass over which she had to pick her way.

Becky was far more fortunate than we in one way: I had carried her dishes and food with us. Only after a nerve-wracking period of driving here and there around neighborhoods that looked deserted (but which we were afraid were *not*) in the rain and darkness did we find a seedy-looking diner where we staved off starvation with greasy hamburgers, sodden home fries, and soft drinks.

The miseries up to that point, it turns out, were only harbingers of what lay ahead. Deb and Becky and I remained inside the motel room the next morning (Deb with a sore throat and still feverish and both of us totally breakfastless) while Don and Holly went to Brooklyn, as arranged, to pick up his parents. What had not been arranged, at least by us, was the thick yellow fog that made any driving a nightmare and completely obliterated signs he depended on in order to follow a maze of streets and bridges on a route totally unfamiliar to him. Of course they got lost—at one point he said he felt he must have died and stepped through the gates of a dark and comfortless netherland—but, hours late, did arrive. With the help of some thinning of the fog, he also got back to pick us up and get to the show, barely in time for Becky's scheduled class.

Deb scarcely remembers going in the ring, and was so weak and shaky she was less pleased than we when the judge did something we have never seen since: After stunning the spectators by awarding our Becky (who had won her class easily) Best-of-Breed from a sizable entry of male and female champions plus the other class winners, he asked Deb to run her charge solo around the entire perimeter of the ring "so that everyone can see what a magnificent Newfoundland bitch looks like."

It was a glorious moment. The class win (the event we had nearly missed getting to in time) had been very gratifying because it had earned Becky her first points toward a championship, but the thrill of winning Breed, topped off by the unusual special display was of historic proportions. Only one other time did we swell with such pride at a dog show: Several years later Becky's son, Shalom, went from his class to win Breed and then on to capture first in the Group.

Becky did not win the Group in the Bronx that day—it would have been nearly unthinkable for any judge to have so ranked a class bitch of any breed—but she was one of the six retained when the judge had excused the twenty or so he did not intend to consider in his final selection.

By the time we collected ourselves to leave, the day was fading, but no faster than we. Holly had become unbearably cross and difficult—behavior we attributed to fatigue and hunger but which, it turned out, were the first symptoms of her malaise. It had been decided that she would go home with her grandparents by subway—Don and Deb and I were to meet Bettye and her friends for dinner at a fancy mid-Manhattan restaurant. None of us felt well, but we chalked it up to fatigue, cold, hunger—and we tried to think in terms of a grand celebration of our marvelous victory.

Holly's celebration didn't wait, however. Her poor grandparents had to cope with the embarrassment and distress that accompanied the literal eruption of her illness in the form of a vomiting siege on the way home. They blamed it on the miserable subway journey, coupled with excitement and exhaustion, just as we blamed Deb's complaints on her sore throat and the upper respiratory infection it was ushering in. Later, however, when I had to bolt from the restaurant table just as our dinners were being served (I spent the next two hours in the parked car with Becky while the rest of the party celebrated—although Deb ate nothing and Don little, so I was told), we decided our repast at the diner the previous evening was quite likely well-laced with microscopic bugs.

The adventure did end. But not without one last lash of the beast's tail. The following morning we all collected at Don's parents' apartment for a breakfast no one wanted and then headed for home. Becky in the back-back was fine. Bettye in the front was in good form—only a bit tired from her fun weekend. Don was grim. He did not feel well but didn't say so. (He had little opportunity between the groans and complaints issuing from the two girls and me, cramped and cross and ill in the back seat.) He just *drove*, with the single-minded purpose of getting us all home.

His efforts bore bitter fruit when, two-tenths of a mile off the four-laner, on the last leg of that seeming endless trip, he was stopped and slapped with a speeding ticket. We were, as noted on the ticket, six miles in excess of the posted limit! At first I thought Don would weep with misery and frustration, but when that pompous state trooper began to scold and asked my long-suffering husband if he didn't think he should show more *concern* for his *family* by driving with more caution, I could feel the blood pressure soar. A more loaded and ominous "Yes, sir" could scarcely have been uttered. I was never quite sure whether the snail's pace at which we traversed the last fifty miles was prompted by the fear of being stopped again or whether Don's fists and knees and toes were so tightly clenched he could not press any harder on the accelerator.

The surprise and joy of our terrific win in the Bronx that long-ago Saturday is with us still. What surprises me even more, when I think about it, is that we went on more dog show weekends *after* that introduction. The fun of the win is intoxicating.

The Inside Story of a Snake

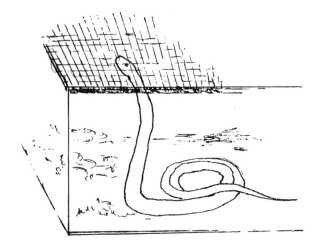

Although dogs and cats have formed the major portion of our family's menageries, we have by no means been so species-limited. We have shared house space with guinea pigs, hamsters, snakes, birds, fish, black "white mice," and—unloved and unwanted by me—seeming hordes of many-legged crawling creatures, all deliberately, if sometimes unwisely, acquired.

Alexander was our first snake. Holly found him on a walk in a nearby ravine, and brought him home with such gentleness and pride, we lacked the heart to tell her then that it was not the thing to do. A naturalist friend of ours, whose aid we enlisted time and again through the years, identified Alexander's "breed" (I've forgotten now but it seems he—or she?—was a "red-bellied" something or other), told us he was harmless, suggested how we might rig a suitable home for him, and described what we should offer him as sustenance. He explained that if the snake didn't learn to take food within a specified length of time, we should free him so he wouldn't die from our attentions.

Don fixed up an old aquarium with dirt, moss, a sunken dish of water to serve both bathing and thirst-quenching needs, and other oddments for the creature's comfort. On the top was a strong wire grill, attached some way or other to the sides of the aquarium.

Alexander loved his condo. He appeared magnificently happy and not only did he eat heartily almost from day one, but he took food directly from Holly's fingers through the openings in the wire top. He liked ground beef okay but clearly preferred his meat alive, so Holly spend hours digging worms or collecting bugs or whatever tidbits we soon discovered he savored. She particularly loved exhibiting to visitors how Alexander "stood up and begged" and then took his rewards from her fingers. True, some adult guests did not seem enchanted—a few were observed to shudder—but many did enjoy the performance. Other children loved it.

Like most parents, Don and I were delighted when our offspring were old enough to be allowed up alone for awhile on Sunday mornings so we could catch some extra sleep. Both of them knew to waken us without hesitation at the slightest problem, so it was no shock when Holly pounced on us very early one Sunday with a demand for assistance. Her message, though, was a jolt. I remember her words precisely: "Mommy, Daddy, come quick! Alexander's there but his insides are gone."

Imagining some gory disembowelment (from what kind of marauder that could have gotten through the mesh of the aquarium top?), we raced to investigate. What we found did indeed look like Alexander "without his insides." Without his *body,* in fact. He had shed his skin in one beautifully intact piece and exited his cage in the process. One square in the wire was slightly spread (by the force he had exerted? or perhaps earlier by fingers poking food through to him?) but was still far smaller than the diameter of Alexander in his normal state. To get through, he must have made himself thinner by half—surely a wonderful trick I'd like to learn— and, I suppose, twice as long? But out he was. Only the skin remained. Not a sign of Alexander was to be found.

The search began. We moved furniture, lifted cushions, emptied boxes of toys, pulled books off shelves, and turned up rugs. He could have *been* anywhere. But he could be *found* nowhere. As the day wore on, we broadened our arena. Could a snake go upstairs? Think of the hiding places! Closets, shoes, beds, chests—the list was endless.

Night came. No Alexander. We sat and we walked with great care. I had a horror of stepping on him, under a rug or bathmat, and an equal horror of seeing a dog or cat appear with a mutilated Alexander in its mouth. We continued to look—for days. A call to our naturalist friend led us to believe Alexander had slipped out an open door (we liked that thought, but had trouble really believing it) or had died from lack of water. In the latter case, we were assured he would probably just dry up and disintegrate without creating a noticeable stench. But we would probably never know.

It was ages before we could really stop looking for Alexander. Our social life suffered, for we did feel obliged to warn guests there was a snake loose in the house, we knew not where or whether alive. Some sat nervously, others remembered they couldn't really stay this time. The lady who helped me clean, poor soul, was nearly in a panic. She was not at all fond of snakes, and, although she had accepted Alexander in his cage with equanimity, she dug dirt from nooks and crannies with considerable trepidation during the weeks after his escape. Bless her dear self, she never failed to come on her appointed days, although she must have dreaded it.

The end of Alexander's tale was almost as much a shock as his escape had been. One fall evening, weeks later, the chill in the air prompted us to inaugurate the fireplace season. Don went to the cellar for logs and kindling, and, as he approached the pile, he saw "sitting" atop it, in his learned food-begging pose, the errant Alexander. Bigger, to be sure, but unmistakably Alexander. And, quite clearly, in the pink of condition. No question he'd found bugs aplenty—probably in the woodpile—and water—lots of damp corners in that old basement.

Although the critter didn't act as if he even wanted to get away, Don pounced on him with all deliberate speed and carried him upstairs. Perhaps Alexander had wondered why we had left him there so long. Back in his cage he went, but a finer mesh topping was added.

The magic was gone, however—for us, if not for Alexander. After several days the entire family escorted him with great ceremony to the ravine from whence he'd come. With pats on the back and fond goodbyes, he was released in the dead leaves at the side of the path—insides *and* skin intact.

Eye of the Beholder

Our career as breeders of Newfoundlands and participants in the dog-show world was brief and meteoric, exploding in an early burst of glory and fading at the same rate. It was enormous fun while it lasted and left us with a series of shining memories. And a few we'd just as soon forget!

We entered the show scene so abysmally ignorant of the process, the purposes, and the rules (written and unwritten) that we can only wonder in retrospect how we avoided making worse fools of ourselves than we did. It seems odd to me that no one, so far as I have been able to discover, has written a concise, simplified description of dog showing, as conducted under the auspices of the American Kennel Club (AKC), without getting enmeshed in a tangle of details and complex rules. The dedicated exhibitor needs to know those, and a true aficionado will want to learn them, but surely others must approach the arena, either as participants or observers, as totally uninformed as we were. They might welcome a basic introduction.

About the only correct assumption we made at the outset was that one entered a dog show so that one might win. Just what was to be won, much less how or why, was a mystery. Of course, win-

ning almost anything is fun and ego-building. Ribbons and trophies are nice. Just participating, without winning, can be fun, and,
for some exhibitors, that is enough. But there is another, more
serious, side to the enterprise.

The bottom-line reason for the holding of such events is the
maintenance and improvement of the various breeds of dogs by
officially designating outstanding examples, thereby acquainting
observers with what constitutes good quality, encouraging the
production of top-quality stock in breeding programs, and helping
those who are doing so by "promoting" and "advertising" their
success.

Viewed in that light, it becomes ridiculously obvious that neutered animals (incapable of reproduction) have no place in a dog
show—a fact that had totally escaped us early on. Assuming as we
did that one put one's dog in a show just for the fun of seeing
whether a judge might think that dog was "better" than other
entrants, it is a minor miracle we didn't commit the cardinal error
of entering our spayed female, our first Newfoundland, in one of
the first events to which we went. Somehow we learned that was
not allowed; only much later did we understand why.

Although that might seem to be the ultimate in naïveté, in our
case it was not. We had not even learned the language, being at that
time unaware that in show or breeding terms, "dog" means male.
A female is properly, and quite casually, referred to as a bitch. Our
children, who, like most well brought-up young people, had heard
the word "bitch" in a less-correct, and certainly less "proper," use,
found it exciting and delightfully naughty to begin tossing the word
around in a confident manner. They also quickly learned the even-
more risqué possibilities of sprinkling their conversations with
various references to "sons-of-bitches."

For the most part, the animals being shown compete only against
others of the same sex, and are divided into "classes"—some for
"dogs," others for bitches. We also learned that all dog (that is, *male*)
classes of one breed are judged first—a concession to the fact that
males could be distracted by "female" scents that might linger in the

ring if the ladies went first. Since animals of both sexes that are already champions *are* judged together, it must be thought that champion males are beyond that sort of thing! At that point in our career, however, we neither grasped the meaning of the term "champion," nor had we any notion how it was attained.

In the beginning, we also completely misunderstood the role of a judge. Although the pragmatism of the process requires the judge to compare, to some extent, the animals in a group ("class") to each other, the specific commitment is to measure how close each animal comes to *perfection*—that is, to compare each real, live dog to the official concept of what a perfect Newfoundland (or German Shepherd, or toy poodle, or any breed) would be. By "official" is meant the "Standard," a written, agreed-upon description of the ideal, or perfect, example of each recognized breed.

Most breed Standards make much of appearance (some critics decry the beauty-contest aspect of dog shows) but almost all deal to some extent with personality and behavior as well, and a good share of the appearance features that are specified relate to health, physical soundness, and other attributes that reflect the animal's capability to fulfill its function. The latter is generally more relevant to those intended for specific jobs, such as the working, sporting, or hound breeds, for example, than to the toy breeds.

Not only is the judge charged with determining which of the dogs being displayed comes closest to the standard of perfection but he or she is to make that determination based only on the evidence available at that time—in *that* ring of *that* show on *that* day. Other knowledge the judge may have—about the blood lines of some of the animals being presented (and, therefore, their potential or lack of it as breeding stock), awareness of how great a certain animal *could* look if groomed properly or presented (handled) well, medical problems one of the dogs may have had that could affect its future use, and so on—is absolutely irrelevant to the judging procedure.

It is vital that exhibitors grasp the what-the-judge-sees-at-this-moment-is-all-that-counts principle, yet it can be one of the least understood and most difficult-to-accept elements. The point was brought home to us quite painfully during and after a dog show in our home town, early in our exhibiting career. We had entered our magnificent bitch, Becky. She was, by all measurements and in nearly all observers' eyes, simply gorgeous. Furthermore, she had already produced outstanding puppies; a few years later, she attained all-time second rank in terms of quality of offspring in the Newfoundland record book.

The judge for Newfs in that show was a woman we knew socially, a factor we knew would in no way influence the decision (for one thing, she had a similar relationship with at least three-quarters of the exhibitors!), but she was familiar with our Becky and had often expressed her delight in, and high opinion of, the dog's superior qualities.

So certain were we of a win and of the chance to "shine" locally that we had painted ourselves into a corner, inviting droves of friends (many of whom had never been to a dog show) to watch the judging and come to our house for drinks afterwards. We barely managed to refrain from *saying* "to celebrate," but it was implied.

A further embellishment to the after-show event would be the guests' opportunity to view Becky's puppies. About eight weeks before, she had whelped a litter and the puppies were, indeed, beautiful. But *Becky* looked *awful*. She was more than half naked (bitches often lose coat after whelping), a bit on the thin side, and out of condition. She was also not at all interested in being shown, and *showed* it. Out of a class of four, Becky took fourth!

We were stung! It would have been hard to find three more pedestrian examples of the breed than her competitors. Yet all were ranked (by a friend!) above our Becky. We were embarrassed. We were furious. The party at our house was somewhat in the nature of a wake.

At a get-together not long after, we were further incensed when our friend, the judge, took us aside and, benevolently but firmly, scolded *us*—for having entered Becky in the show. She pointed out that it was a disservice—to the dog, to other exhibitors, (and, unstated but implied, to herself), to the audience, and to ourselves—to have displayed such a normally beautiful creature looking the way she did that day.

Our friend was quite willing to concede that Becky was a far finer animal than those to whom first, second, and third places had been awarded. She told us furthermore, that had she been asked to choose one of the four bitches to add to her own kennel stock, Becky would have been the hands-down winner, but that that choice would have been made on the basis of her personal knowledge of the dog, and most certainly not on what she saw in the ring that day.

We did, at last, understand. It would, of course, make no sense to be otherwise. For one thing, it would be grossly unfair if judges were to carry outside knowledge into the ring, where they are often confronted by some animals they know well alongside others they have never seen before. It would also be utterly misleading to observers not familiar with the breed if judges were to rank poor-appearing specimens over their better-looking competitors.

Having finally grasped that point, we were also able to understand the importance of good grooming and correct handling. If the dog is not properly groomed and is not presented well enough for the judge and everyone else to *see* its good qualities, how can it be awarded honors for those qualities?

We had learned a couple of painful lessons. We still had a long way to go.

Special Delivery

Babies pick the darndest times to be born. Ask any obstetrician. Ask any mother! Actually most mothers I've known don't really seem to care a whole lot about the time of day or day of the week or anything much except getting the job done once the time has come. I used to do a lot of work for an equine reproductive laboratory; among other tasks, I wrote up for lay readers the staff's projects and research results. It didn't take long in poring over their records and notes to discover that mares too apparently deliver their foals most often during the hours when sensible creatures sleep. It helped explain the usual heavy-lidded, yawning, weary countenances of many of the graduate students and other workers there.

It must be a plot—maybe it's just Mother Nature taking her fun where she can find it—because puppies too seem to like the off hours, or else the most hectic or inconvenient circumstances, in which to make their debuts. In our limited experience, the scenario usually called for me to be up all of one night, alert to what seemed an imminent delivery, and then, when exhaustion began to take its toll and all the other demands of life and family arrived in a rush with the morning, *then* the puppies would begin to appear. The few times when that was not the schedule, there were other elements that conspired to upset the program which had been thoroughly anticipated and for which we had tried to plan during the previous nine weeks.

Nothing, however, could top 'Sicha's performance in just about every endeavor. For the first couple of years of her life we had become convinced she was put on earth for no other purpose than to bedevil us. Selected as the choicest prospect from Becky's "Seven-Sisters" litter: (seven puppies total, all female), to be Holly's very own—to train, to show, and later to breed—she repeatedly upset our apple carts. Healthy and well-balanced but too small and totally undramatic to show well, she ruined not only Holly's chance to take a dog to its championship but spoiled one of Becky's possible records: To this day, 'Sicha remains the only one of Becky's offspring ever to be shown and *not* become a champion. With enough effort, it might have been done, but Holly (and the rest of us) found it too discouraging to keep bringing home those "Reserve" ribbons. Taking "Reserve" in a dog show is a lot like being a bridesmaid—once or twice is fun, but "always" and "only" is not.

Disappointing as her performance in the ring was, it was scarcely cause for banishment. Her refusal to be fenced in was. And so, when our every effort to keep her confined, and the limits of our patience, had been thoroughly tested and found wanting, we turned (as we so often did) to our good friends, Helena and Bill Linn, for rescue. "Do something with her," we pleaded. "Find a buyer, *give* her away, get her off our hands somehow."

Now, Bill and Helena were no fools. They were more than aware of the blood lines and the marvelous pool of genes packaged in that renegade runt and of the fact that, bred to the right male, she could easily turn out to be a super brood bitch. Which, of course, she did. And, at that stage of their outstanding kennel reputation, brood bitches were useful, another championship was not. Besides, their facilities (and their smarts) were far better suited to keeping her home than ours.

So Ganshalom's Nesicha Shomeret became an Edenglen resident. (We took, in her place, the lovely Shir Hashirim, "Song of Songs.") And did she ever become a brood bitch! The Linns had, over the years, shipped puppies to buyers in every corner of the U.S.A., and some beyond, but 'Sicha's babies turned out to be super international jet-setters. Males especially were destined to play key roles in breeding programs in places as far apart as Denmark and Australia. Female babies became foundation bitches for several domestic kennels. But that part of 'Sicha's history had yet to be realized.

At the time the little devil pulled her last trick on us, she was already living at Edenglen, was not quite four years old, had had one litter for the Linns the previous September, and was expecting her second early in April. A Newfoundland Specialty Show was held on the last day of March that year in Buffalo, and we were showing our Shalom. The Linns were to be there too; I believe Bill and Helena were playing a special role in the proceedings—Bill may have been judging some of the classes, but I'm not positive of that.

Buffalo was one of those show sites that always presented us with a dilemma: too far to go there and back in one day, with the long hours and tiring activity of a show sandwiched in between, yet too close to easily justify the greatly added expense of our staying overnight, *and* the kenneling of other dogs to make overnight trips possible. That time, we decided to make it one—long, long—day. Don, Holly, Shalom, and I must have been up and on the road long before dawn, so we chose to forego the evening show festivities and left Buffalo, already exhausted, late in the afternoon.

We hadn't had the marvelous boost to energy and endurance that winning brings, so it was a bushed bunch that gratefully tumbled out of the old station wagon in the carport at home. We managed to grab a bite to eat, the dogs at home and Shalom were fed and watered and petted a bit, and the car was mostly unloaded but not cleaned at all. Clumps of dog hairs, the filthy blanket in the back that had caught masses of mud and snow and rain and grit from Newfie riders over the preceding months, a couple of grungy towels used to mop up dog drool—all were left for the morrow. Because Holly had passed up some event to which she and her then-current boyfriend had been invited that day, she was barely home before rushing off to meet him and other friends to catch up on whatever she had missed.

During the day we had visited briefly with the Linns and checked on news of 'Sicha. Only a few more days until her puppies are due, they said. Yes, all the dogs were being looked after by Freddy, a neighbor of theirs whom we'd met; no he wasn't staying at their house but would be coming three times that day and again the next morning (the Linns *were* staying overnight since show duties would keep them there until midnight); he would feed and water and clean runs and check on everything; etc.

Although I assumed their house would be closed and empty, I knew they had a telephone in the barn, and just before I was ready to crawl into bed (Don was already sound asleep), I decided to give that phone a ring. I can't really imagine why. Newfoundlands are more like people than people are sometimes, but I've yet to meet one who could answer a phone. And there was no imaginable reason to expect Freddy to be there—in the barn at 10 P.M.

No imaginable reason? Truth is, I devoutly hoped not. Because the only reasons would be bad ones: A sick or injured dog? A bitch in labor earlier than expected? (Dogs' gestation periods and delivery dates are quite predictable—obviously knowing the exact dates of probable conception are a help on that score—so even a few days' variance from expectation is fairly unusual.)

I dialed the phone. It rang. No one—of course!—answered. Until, on about the sixth or seventh ring as I relaxed and was about to hang-up, a breathless, eager voice blurted out "Hello!" Oh yes, it was Freddy. Oh yes, 'Sicha was having puppies. Good God, all hell was breaking loose! One puppy had arrived, and 'Sicha had the infant in her mouth. She would not let Freddy have it, nor would she put it down where it could cuddle up to her for warmth and nourishment but simply carried it around and around the stall in the barn where she was confined. The non-heated barn was freezing cold, the house was locked.

My suggestions, made in a series of telephone calls back and forth, proved of little help. Freddy did turn on the heating lamp he had found and put it in 'Sicha's stall, but the new mother didn't want "that fellow" coming near her baby and wasn't about to change her mind about yielding the puppy to him so he could put it near the heat.

Between calls to and from Freddy, I located Holly at a friend's house, woke Don to jabber the news at him that she and I were going to Edenglen, and grabbed my handbag and the keys to the car. With utter stupidity I simply raced to the car and took off to collect Holly and head for the scene of action some thirty miles away. Just a few more minutes and I could have grabbed rags, towels, suitable clothing for Holly, food or drink—a dozen other useful items.

Although the road was icy in spots, we got there without mishap, but not before another baby had arrived. 'Sicha was alternately carrying the first one and then the second. At any given moment, one was in danger of freezing since both puppies were soaking wet from birth fluids and saliva, and both needed nourishment. Clearly, 'Sicha was absolutely unwilling to let Freddy touch either puppy.

One look and Holly climbed the barrier into the stall, put out her hands, and said, " 'Sicha, *give!*" A soft soggy puppy was gently placed in her palms by an obviously relieved mother. One more command, "Down," and, within seconds, Holly had two babies vigorously sucking warm milk into their bellies, while she and I rubbed them with the only thing we could find—crumpled newspapers. Rags, towels, and all the other paraphernalia needed for attending a bitch and newborn puppies—and for keeping the human attendants warm and comfortable too!—were securely locked inside the owners' house. (It seems the young man had been told where the key was, but he had forgotten.)

It was a very long, very cold, very sleepless night. From our arrival, around midnight, until post-sunup the next morning we delivered puppies. Freddy had gratefully taken himself home to bed shortly after we got there, promising to be back early the next morning. But, again, how had I been so stupid as to let him go without asking for some needed items from his house? I was not functioning at my most-organized best!

We were not busy every minute, of course, but there was never any way to predict the intervals between arrivals. Sometimes it was as little as fifteen minutes—scarcely time to get a puppy half-way dry and nursing—sometimes more than an hour. 'Sicha, naturally, slept peacefully between clusters of contractions. Why not? We were taking care of things, and she didn't look ahead anyway. Several times Holly crawled into the rear seat of our wagon and, huddling under the dirty, hairy dog blanket, caught a few minutes' sleep. Her eyes were seldom closed long, however, before I'd yell again for help. I lay down once in the car, so tired I thought I *had* to rest. But it was bitterly cold—and there was too little gasoline to be sure we could get back home if we ran the engine to warm the car.

Once an umbilical cord was bitten incompletely by a tiring and increasingly unenthusiastic mother dog, and I had no way to sever it properly until Holly dug frantically in a tool box on the barn's workbench and produced the only cutting instrument she could find—a rusty, dirty, *dull* linoleum knife. With it, we managed to get the cord separated, and nobody bled to death.

'Sicha was not the only one losing her enthusiasm. The puppies came. And came. And came. Six or seven was often thought to be a fairly standard litter, although there was considerable variation. 'Sicha had produced seven babies the first time around, which was a pretty hefty number for a debut. It soon became clear that that had been just a warm-up for the future. That night she had a couple dozen. Well—of course, she didn't really. It just seemed like it! Actually, Holly and I both remember the count as eleven. We know one died—we tried hard to keep it alive but the task was hopeless, and a later examination showed it to have had a defect that prevented it from nursing so it could not have lived. Still, we were *sure* there were either eleven with it or eleven besides. According to the registration records, however, there were not quite that many, so perhaps we did hallucinate. Or—I wonder. Did some play a revolving-door trick on us and make multiple entrances? I would believe almost anything of that night.

Unfortunately the last puppy in a litter never arrives with a sign saying "This is it"—one must wait several hours to be sure. By the time we felt confident we were at the end of the line, the babies were warm and dry and had taken nourishment several times, 'Sicha was cleaned up as much as we could manage and had had a turn in the exercise yard (escorted by us peering through the dark to try to make sure she didn't deposit another puppy out there), and we were delighted to hear the sound of Freddy's car coming down the hill.

By the time he got there, he had a lot to do. All the dogs were long awake and clamoring for food, as, for sure, was 'Sicha. We gratefully left him to his tasks. Later that day we heard from the Linns that all was well with the whole crew including the new additions. Bill and Helena were, of course, grateful for our help— and expressed their thanks to excess with the gift of one of Bill's gorgeous hand-made hooked rugs. It has a Newf in black against a bright red background, and I did *not* divide it with Holly. She had done her share indeed—right up to our departure. Then she conked out on the back seat and slept all the way home.

I almost did—it took me two-and-one-half hours to make thirty or so miles. Even with windows wide open to the frigid air and the radio blaring, my eyes kept closing. Three times I think I dropped off simultaneously with getting the car off the road and stopped. I awoke several times with my head on the steering wheel without any clear memory of parking or turning off the key. In between naps, I drove at a snail's pace for fear of yielding suddenly to the urge to sleep.

Well, it *had* been a long session—we had left home in March and here it was April by the time we got back. April first—April Fool's Day. Indeed! The eternal jokester, 'Sicha.

All Good Things

All the four-legged friends I've loved and lost were mourned and are missed, but none ever owned my heart as totally and forever as 'Sammy. Her full name was Ganshalom's Shachor Kasam—the latter pronounced "Kah-Psalm," to rhyme with "palm," or "balm." We spelled it " 'Sam." More than sixty years I've lived, and the darkest day of all, so far, was the one when I said my last goodbye to 'Sammy.

What makes one creature, in all tangible and outward ways almost identical to others of her ilk, stand out as uniquely splendid? In 'Sammy's case, her specialness no doubt reflected to a large extent the uniqueness of the circumstances. She was the last of our breeding, the one we'd kept from the final litter born to our kennel. And, because she outlived all her litter mates, she was the last dog to bear the Ganshalom prefix in her name. But she was special long before then.

I never parted easily with any dog with which I'd shared house room. I wept at the departure of each puppy, even though they went at only eight or nine weeks of age, and then into the happy homes of good people. When various circumstances forced me to place adult dogs outside our home, often to their benefit, I had all I could do to endure the separation. But 'Sammy was the one I could *not* part with. She had claimed me beyond recall when she was less than four weeks old.

Wanting to keep one bitch for anticipated future breeding from that January 1975 litter (which we did not know was to be our last), I had studied the six females in the over-large group of eleven with my most objective eye. By the time they were three weeks old, it seemed there were two clear leaders in the field. I marked each with the usual dab of nail polish on the head for closer observation.

To ease the drain on the dam of feeding such a large litter, we started the puppies on supplemental food earlier than normal. Watching them at the food pans was not only, as usual, the way to be sure all were getting their fair shares, but provided one of the best opportunities for assessing the quality of individual pups. In this situation, the two marked ones were the prime targets of my observation. Or, I meant them to be. But one of the unmarked pups—another little "girl"—had a different idea. She opted for love over food. Although she approached the pans in the eager, clumsy, tumble-all-over-each-other-and-even-into-the-gruel manner of the whole galloping crew, the minute *I* stepped back from the milling mob, *she* followed. She would climb all over my feet and legs, looking up, rolling her eyes in adoration, and beg with every atom of her little furry body to be held and cuddled.

Time after time, I'd plunk her back into the crowd, pointing her nose into the glop, but no more than a lap or two would she take before turning away again for my attentions. She made it clear she would rather be fondled than fed, rather give love than get sustenance. It was my 'Sammy, stealing my heart for all time.

Already the smallest of the litter, if she were not to starve, I had no choice but to stand beside her, petting and encouraging her to eat. Soon, I was putting her food in a special dish and taking her apart from the others to eat. An unbreakable bond was forged. Without ever consciously making the decision, all the others were soon "on the market," and one-by-one, they were placed in their new homes. Even 'Sam's mother soon went, for various practical reasons, to the home of friends, owners of another kennel who could cope with the prolific reproduction of which she had proved herself so capable. In exchange, we took a male puppy from 'Sicha, a Ganshalom bitch we had placed with them when our efforts to fence her in had failed. Melech, as he was named, and 'Sammy—almost identical in age—grew up together as "the kids" along with Shalom "the old man," and "Aunt" Tari, a young female we acquired soon after Melech arrived. Shalom died when "the kids" were less than a year old, and by then we were making plans to move west, so we kept our collection to the three: Tari, Melech, and 'Sam.

Our hope had been to move the three with us, but when our plans were finalized, it became clear that only one could go. I wanted to give Melech to Holly ('Sicha had been her dog, and it seemed fitting that 'Sicha's son should be hers), but Holly was living in a trailer and could not take him. I had also hoped to send Tari to Deb, but Deb and her husband were living in a rented house where they were not allowed to have pets.

We faced a terrible decision: two of the dogs that had been part of our family *for four years,* had to be sent to other homes. Never, except by death, had I had to part with animals I'd shared that much of my life with. It was an agonizing time but there was no alternative. Nor was the choice ever in doubt. Not only was 'Sammy irrevocably bound to me by the events of her first weeks, but I doubted that anyone anywhere would spend the effort and the time, not to mention the large sums of money, required to battle her ongoing health problems.

The wrench in "abandoning" Melech and Tari—which was what I felt we were doing, despite the promising homes we found for them—left permanent scars I still can scarcely bear to touch. To have parted from 'Sammy would have been utterly unbearable.

Our new life and home in Seattle were so delightful that regrets were very few and far between. I did find it odd to have *one dog* and did, indeed, miss my "gang" (and ached for the uprooted two we left behind), but I discovered the joys of sharing all my hours with a special pet. For the first time in years, my work was done almost entirely in my office at home. 'Sammy was always on the floor beside my desk. Because of her penchant for consuming anything she could get her mouth around, every time I went out—to the library, shopping, the dentist, visiting—she went in the car with me. When I cooked, she lay on the floor in the kitchen (hoping I'd drop something!); when we slept, she slept beside the bed. Except for a few brief periods each day for necessary duties in her exercise yard, she was never more than a few feet from my side.

At no other time in my life had I had as intense and prolonged a relationship with one animal. We had almost always had two or more, I had often worked away from home, and there had, for most of the previous years, been one or both of the children at home, "diluting" individual person-dog interactions. In addition to the quantitative element of 'Sammy's and my togetherness, there was the special qualitative aspect engendered by her allergy problems. Various kinds of maintenance medications and treatments were required several times a day, flare-ups of a more acute nature punctuated the routine with the need for additional care—and always there was watching for trouble, and worrying.

One of the most incredible aspects of 'Sammy's story is, nevertheless, her *good* health. *She lived longer, by several years, than any other Newfoundland we ever had.* And, perhaps more remarkable yet, except for the allergies and allergically triggered ailments, she had been sick only once in her life—a temporary front-leg lameness—until her final illness.

That illness took us by surprise. After years of trying to brace ourselves for what we had expected to be an early death, we must finally have come to believe in her immortality. With the allergies under good control for several years, her aging appeared to be such a natural process, such a gradual slowing, that it was scarcely discernible.

From the first faint alarm that all might not be right until the end was just one week. She had been kenneled the previous week, and when we got her home, she seemed to sleep excessively even for her. Snoozing is not an uncommon state for Newfoundlands—

certainly not for those with no companion dogs to stimulate them and most especially not for one of her age and stage of life. Besides, we assumed that life at the kennel was less than tranquil and that she was just plain tired. All by itself, the extra napping would have rung no major bells.

A shiver of apprehension did creep over us as we listened to her chronic cough, although it was almost as routine for her as the tendency to sleep a lot. She had coughed in the same way—a dry, soft, non-explosive procedure—for years. Because it resembled the cough that can be a sign of heart trouble, it had been repeatedly checked out. Each time, the diagnosis was that it was nothing more than another manifestation of her many allergies. Now, however, it seemed worse—more frequent, deeper, harsher—so, after a day or two, we took her to the doctor.

'Sammy's throat, it turned out, was red and looked mildly inflamed. Could be, the veterinarian said, that she had a slight upper-respiratory infection (no fever or other signs to indicate so, but still a possibility) and that could be the cause of the cough. Or, and here we failed to note the potentially ominous implications, the throat redness and inflammation could be the *result*, not the cause, of the increased coughing. A course of antibiotics was prescribed to deal with the infection that might be there. Within a day or two, the cough had abated, and 'Sammy had perked up. All looked to be on the mend.

Then the red-flag event occurred: I looked out one morning to see 'Sammy lying down beside her half-full dish of breakfast. Her voracious and uncontrollable appetite was so pronounced a feature of her existence that I had often said "If she ever refuses food, I'll know she's dying."

Back we went to the veterinarian—a good fellow who may then have suspected the worst or who may have simply wanted to make absolutely sure the best available care was given to this well-loved creature. At any rate he suggested we get her without delay to a specialist, an internist he knew (and whom we knew slightly) some fifty miles away.

We took her that afternoon, of course. She was examined. We talked at length with the doctor. She had radiographs. The doctor showed them to us and discussed possibilities. He suggested she be left overnight for observation, for more tests, and for an endoscopic examination of the respiratory system. The latter would have to be done under anesthesia, always a risk and especially so at 'Sammy's age. The trip home without her seemed long. It would be longer the next day.

The following morning, the anesthesia and the endoscopy were accomplished without a hitch, but shortly after, the heartbreaking verdict was in. Cancer. Inoperable, untreatable lung cancer.

We got the news in a telephone call at noon, and, within moments, we knew it was over. 'Sammy would not come home again. Don heard me talk and saw me struggle with the option to bring her back and wait. How long? Two days? A week? As she faded? As she lost all joy in life? As, quite likely, the pain began? And then? The arguments in my head were as short-lived as 'Sammy's hours were destined to be. The letting go could not be delayed. We drove north in stunned and sorrowing silence to say our farewell.

I held dear 'Sammy in my arms and smoothed the silky coat along her head and throat while I spoke to her of all the joy she had given us. I thanked her for her loving life, so generously given to our keeping. I wished her peace and told her to go to sleep, and nodded to the doctor to give the merciful injection. 'Sammy was looking at me as the light went out of her eyes. A light went out in my heart forever.

Mess Call

Call somebody a chowhound and there is little doubt what you mean. The person probably belongs more to the live-to-eat than the eat-to-live club. Most dogs I've known earned that label for they generally ate just about anything, anytime, they could. Yet canine attitudes toward food apparently vary as much as people's do, and I am told that some pets drive their owners crazy by refusing to eat or turning up their noses at anything other than a few specialty items of their own selection.

The closest we ever came to that kind of finickiness was with Becky during the latter half of a pregnancy. Then we went to no end of trouble tempting her to take in sufficient nourishment for herself and the family she was carrying. We have lived with almost every other level of food interest-disinterest at one time or another. Kasam and Samantha top our list of foodies—both displaying what could only be considered true addiction to oral consumption. Neither one really ate; they engulfed their food. Since Kasam's was a drug-induced approach, Samantha should be given top honors in that category. She ate anything, especially if I was fixing it for people. Raw onions, olives, potato peelings—it didn't matter. Whenever I cut into a cantaloupe, one of her dearest favorites, she could smell it three rooms away and would go into an ecstasy of anticipation. Poor baby, she lived hungry, tended to obesity and had to be put on reducing diets frequently, and died of a terrible ailment related to ingestion and digestion.

Although gastric torsion (and the fatal bloat it often causes) is not restricted to overeaters (Becky died of the same dreadful thing) it seemed unusually ironic that dear Samantha was done in by her stomach. I had often expressed the wish that I could know ahead of time when she was to die so I could let her, just *once*, eat all she wanted. Her last meal, though, was but a meager handful of dry food, lightly moistened. For more than a year she had had only such snacks, five or six times a day, to try to prevent a repeat of her first bout of torsion. She had been rescued from it barely in time, and in spite of all precautions did not survive the second.

Shauna approaches the other end of the appetite spectrum. Most of the time she eats the meal she is given and appears to enjoy it moderately. But if something even mildly interesting—a bird landing on the terrace nearby, a dog barking in a neighbor's yard—happens while she is eating, she leaves the food dish immediately to investigate. Sometimes she doesn't even bother to go back and finish. Now and then she looks at a pan of food I have just put down—in the usual place at the usual time—and look up at me as if to say "What is that for?" And then wanders off to sniff the grass or stare at the sky or ponder the pond. The first few times that happened was shortly after she came to us and immediately following our loss of Kasam whose appetite was legendary, and I was terribly frightened that Shauna was ill and about to die too. Now I know that food is simply not an exciting part of her life.

Shauna does like tidbits from the table but she is not a beggar. She almost never bothers people while they eat, sometimes taking an inquiring sniff if someone is munching on a snack away from the dining table but backing off immediately if told to. In former years, I have had to literally work across the backs and noses of many of our dogs to prepare food in the kitchen; Shauna lies quietly out of the path of action, showing no interest unless something drops on the floor. Even then she is much less likely to make a leaping dive, as 'Sammy and others did, often ignoring bits and pieces that might fall until I have finished and stepped away. Then she becomes the good broom a pet should be, sweeping up all crumbs with a delicate, methodical touch of the tongue to each.

But, oh how she does beg for ordinary dog biscuits! I cannot believe they are that good; yet, for some reason they represent for her the ultimate treat. She knows exactly where they are kept, upstairs and down, and whenever we are near either cupboard she expresses her yearning in language so intense it is near irresistible. At such times, she sits facing the appropriate cupboard, every atom of her one-hundred-forty pounds held in a tight, tense stillness of concentration that is a marvel to behold. Nothing moves—even her breathing seems to cease—except her magnificent eyes. Those glorious dark pools, just rimmed with pearly whiteness, dart with rhythmic precision back and forth from cupboard door to human face, to door to face, to door, and on and on and on.

I cannot stand and watch. I must either reach for a biscuit to break the spell or walk away. Her requests are so frequent and so unbearably eloquent that, to protect both of us, I have determined a specific number of biscuits per day that may be dispensed. I steel myself at other times to pat her on the head, remind her "You know this is not biscuit time," and turn my back. She *does* know, and never pursues the matter beyond the expected response. Still, there have been those instances when (for who knows what reason?) I have unexpectedly yielded. It's always worth a try!

As anyone who has ever lived with them knows, dogs catch on to routine quickly and appear to take comfort from it. That penchant for learning from methodical repetition is what makes training and dependable behavior possible. When we had several Newfs, I used to line up the food dishes on the drainboard of the large, old-fashioned sink in the dog room and prepare all the meals at once. Although more or less the same, the quantities fed to each were often different and additives to the basic diet varied too. A pregnant bitch or growing puppy got extra supplements, some adult dogs could handle certain table scraps without stomach upsets while others could not, and some seemed to do more chewing (better for the teeth) on a drier mix while others gulped either.

I always brought the entire gang inside while I fixed their meals, because they seemed to derive so much pleasure from the anticipation. It was a noisy business—the clatter of metal pans coming off the shelf and being set down on the porcelain, the crunch of the scoop going into the kibble, the rumble as the dry food was dumped into one pan after another, the clang of the metal lid being slammed back on the storage can, the creak of the can opener grinding its way around the top of tinned food, the whack of the fork as gobs of canned meat were plunked into each dish, and the whoosh of the refrigerator door as tidbits and leftovers were extracted. Every sound sent tremors of excitement coursing though already quivering black bodies. Eagerness prompted much bouncing on behinds too, for the dogs were required to sit during the process. (Lying down would have been acceptable had any of them ever had the calmness to try it.)

When at last the water was turned on and the swish of stirring portions was heard, one or another of the waiting beasties sometimes got carried away and rose up, plunking paws down on sink edge or drainboard. Such action brought a sharp rebuke, however, because that kind of behavior was highly contagious and had the potential to incite a riot.

Holly often helped me feed, and she could get by with far more changes in routine. She used to hand out one or two dry kibbles to each as an hors d'oeuvre, and managed to do so without upsetting the demeanor of all. Sometimes she did the feeding chore alone, and taught her 'Sicha to lick the fork used to scoop out the canned food. Most dogs would have hurt their mouths on the tines (spoons offered for a lick were sometimes chomped down on so forcefully they bent). 'Sicha not only learned to lick the fork safely but to take bites of food presented on it, exactly as a person does, enclosing it between upper jaw and tongue and sliding the food off with her lips. Holly loved to show that trick off to visitors.

When all the dishes were ready they were carried outside and placed for eating. But no random process, that. Since I never grew the extra hands I often wished I had and a tray just didn't seem quite the thing, only two orders could be put out at once. Each animal had his or her special spot for eating—the pans were placed roughly in a circle so the diners' tails pointed toward the center with the faces outward (privacy, of a sort!). Each dish was planted against a fence or large stone so they wouldn't keep "walking" away propelled by lapping tongues. The order of service was precise too. Through the years there were changes, depending on what dogs we had at the time but, as long as she lived, Samantha got her food last. And as long as she lived, she still finished first!

As each two dishes were put down, the appropriate dogs began to eat (no attempt was made to have them hold back for a simultaneous start!) but the action of those that were waiting varied. Samantha, even when the poor thing was old and badly crippled, chugged in and out with each and every set of pans—perhaps she hoped someday to get a first one and then the last one also. Others waited inside near the filled dishes, and still others outside at their eating places until dinner arrived.

Sometimes one dog would lick another's pan when the owner had finished and walked away, but I always monitored the diners at their meals in order to notice any changes in eating patterns, so the dishes were usually collected too quickly for much of that. There were dogs that never seemed to bother with the search for leftovers, obviously content with their allotted portion and secure in the fact that another meal would be forthcoming at the appropriate time.

Because routine figures so strongly in dogs' behavior, owners must beware of inadvertently teaching what they do not mean to. At one point when Shauna was refusing enough meals to worry me, I stumbled by accident on part of the problem. Without realizing it, I had, it seems, established a rigid pattern: I mixed her food, opened the door for both of us to go through, carried out the food dish and placed it in the exact same spot on the terrace, patted her on the head and then the rump, and said "There you go." In the spring when the ducks had recently returned to our pond, I sometimes looked to see if they were there for *their* breakfast and apparently forgot the pats and the "There you go." It seems she was waiting for that signal that it was all right to eat!

Once I recognized the problem, I religiously followed the expected routine for several days (and she ate); then I began gradually to mix up the procedure, adding and changing words until I had broken the spell attached to that one special set of stage business.

The incident reminded me of a similar, but worse, situation from my youth, nearly fifty years before. At that time, I had a dog, the first of my very own and the only purebred animal anyone in our family had owned. That black cocker, named Quita, was my absolute pride and joy. She was allowed to run loose—no one I knew thought of fencing or otherwise confining a dog in those days—and I worried. Not only were there cars and trucks (although far fewer than we live with now) but deliberate poisoning was, alas, not a particularly rare event. People who tend to romanticize earlier days, viewing them as gentler times, might change their minds if they were to live awhile in that world. The method of choice for ridding one's property of unwanted canine or feline trespassers was to put out a lump of hamburger well-laced with strychnine. I determined to protect Quita from such an eventuality by teaching her to never, never take anything into her mouth without my permission.

It is highly doubtful whether my plan would have proved an adequate safeguard anyway. The training at which I spent so much time and effort would probably have been considered irrelevant by Quita on the roam, but it worked at home—too well. She had, at last, over many weeks been taught to leave her food dish, even temptingly full, absolutely untouched until I gave her the appropriate command. So stringent were my lessons that she was sometimes made to wait up to an hour before being allowed to eat a meal that was in full view and accessible. I enlisted other family members to test her by giving her the same signal I used—and then rebuked her if she so much as made a move towards the dish. It would be good if I now took the time and care to teach worthwhile behavior to my pets as rigorously as I undertook that misguided mission.

For that was the summer just before I was to go away to college. My mother, who had paid little attention along the way to that effort as to all of what she considered my "nonsense about that dog," suddenly paused one day to observe what was going on and said with her usual acidity, "Is Quita to eat then only when you are home on vacation?" I was dumbstruck, and not the least part at my own stupidity. For the remaining two weeks before I left, a crash course to end all was mounted, and my poor little doggie unlearned the lessons in time to survive. And, thank goodness, was never poisoned intentionally or otherwise.

It is difficult for me to conceive that anyone could deliberately offer any creature food that is known to be toxic and intended to harm. From the first taste of milk at the mother's breast, the process of eating is one of sterling trust. To me, giving of food to anyone at any age should be an expression of love.

A Fishy Bowl Story

Okay, I admit it. I'm a species bigot. I understand something about the balance of nature, and I find the notion enchanting that all God's creatures are equal, but the truth is I think some are more equal than others. It has something to do with legs. No legs is all right by me—I rather like snakes, in fact—and either two or four is okay too, although I tend to prefer the quadrupeds, but more than four gets just too crawly for charm. There are exceptions—bees, looking like miniature flying teddy bears, are favorites of mine, and some moths and butterflies, for all their six legs, look more like airborne flowers than insects—but most of the rest of the many-legged creatures have to manage without my love.

And I detest spiders. Indeed, I am—or, at any rate, was—a full-fledged, psychologist-diagnosed spiderphobic. Even after extensive treatment for my affliction, their very *name* gives me the creeps. I cannot help thinking the world would be a vastly improved place if it were to limp along somehow without those abominable beasts. If I had the means, I would happily zap forever all spiders, and if my powers extended that far, I would be sorely tempted to do away with cockroaches too. And fleas. Maybe a few others. Would the balance of nature really be so upset thereby that our world would tip on its axis and all of the rest of us be left hanging by our fingernails or toenails? (I wonder if insects have toenails?)

Like most bigots, though, I'm basically ashamed of my prejudices, so maybe I was trying to hide them, or maybe I was trying for the all-time motherhood medal, but I did manage to conceal from the kids my panic at the mere sight of an eight-legged creeper. Too well! Deb, until she was older and learned to despise spiders on her own, didn't seem to care much about them one way or another. But Holly! Holly thought they were *cute!*

At the age of about four or five she became fascinated by all crawling critters. It may have started with an ant farm someone gave her as a birthday present. I found little to thrill me about that addition to our family, but sealed-in as they were in the ingeniously designed contraption, I was able to cope quite well. Not so the others she began collecting, enclosed less securely in makeshift containers of her or her father's devising. But my worst moments involved the spiders.

I get chills remembering how I used to sit with Don on our sunporch, renovated to serve as a sort of family recreation room, watching—or trying to watch—television when the corners of both my eyes were riveted in horrible fascination on an old fish bowl converted to spider house. Never did its residents cease in their efforts to squeeze between the rim of the bowl and the piece of glass laid across the top as a lid. I kept wishing that fish bowl could revert magically to its former use in the children's playroom of our previous house.

Speaking of the children's playroom brings a smile to my lips, for at least two reasons. One, because far from being the spacious residence the existence of such a room suggests, the house was painfully small. Four rooms—living room, dining room, kitchen, and "master" bedroom—were an identical eleven and a half feet square. Two other rooms where the girls slept were so tiny they scarcely could be called bedrooms. One barely held a single bed, small chest, and a couple of orange crates. (About half our furniture consisted of orange crates painted or skirted or otherwise covered and used as end tables, bookcases, toy cupboards, filing cabinets, canned goods storage, and whatever.) The smallest room was not a *bed*room at all because it could accommodate only a crib, not even a single bed. Neither room had a closet; a bracket on the back of the door served as the place to hang clothing.

For all its less-than-one-thousand total square footage, that little house boasted an entry foyer, small to be sure. When the front door was opened it just cleared the bottom of the rather steep stairs that rose straight ahead. Immediately beyond the top step was the door to the bathroom, and inside, facing the door, in direct line of sight of anyone entering the house, was the toilet. In a house with small children, keeping a bathroom door closed even when in use is tough enough; keeping it closed at other times is hopeless. So every visitor to our house in those years was instantly treated to a view of the toilet. When they were lucky, it was unoccupied.

Because there was simply nowhere else to store toys or to use them, we turned the dining room into a playroom and learned to enjoy our meals in a corner of the kitchen or buffet style in either the living room or dining-room-turned-playroom.

The second reason I smile when I think of that playroom is that it did that to people. It was delightful. On the floor, we put linoleum with a gray background and a red-yellow-blue spatter-paint pattern. Along the main wall, under the room's two windows, Don created a wonderfully large play table of plywood atop a series of—yes, more orange crates—which held games and toys. Crates and plywood, and a bench Don's father built, were painted a bright blue. With sunny yellow walls, an old rollaway bed covered in bright red seersucker, and cafe curtains in a red, white, and blue print, the room was charming.

The rollaway bed served as our only guest quarters, and some of our adult friends who spent a night or two with us said they woke up feeling like children again. That sensation was no doubt helped along by the paintings Don did on the walls. Beside the door to the kitchen, with feet (in giant funny shoes) just resting on the top of a small stool we kept there, "stood" a life-size clown, holding a bunch of variously colored balloons, one of which touched the ceiling. His wonderful happy face—with thick-lipped, bright-red mouth, huge eyes, and bulbous nose—would have brought a smile to the dourest Scrooge. How the children hated to leave that clown when we bought a larger house and moved.

On one end of the play table was the large glass fish bowl I'd found at a rummage sale. It had a good-sized crack we'd mended with melted paraffin, a seal that seemed to work okay except that, whenever I cleaned the bowl, I had to reseal it. The goldfish that called it home for years didn't seem to mind. Nor did they try to escape as they might have by emulating their leaping, brightly colored peers painted on the wall above their bowl.

Stranger yet, they never seemed to mind that the cats, Henrietta and Jo-Jo, made the bowl their water dish. I suppose the cats must have liked the fishy taste of the water because, as long as the fish bowl was there, they never drank from any other container, yet not once did they carry that appetite the obvious next step and eat a fish.

The fish were not in the least afraid of those lapping pink tongues (or the feline faces attached to them, looming over the top of the bowl), but actually appeared to be attracted to the cats' tongues and would swim right up to the darting pink appendages. Jo-Jo, always a shy cat, would pull back in alarm if a fish came near; Henrietta ignored them, occasionally even flipping over a curious one that came too close.

If the water in the fish bowl got so low it was hard to reach without leaning so far into the cavity that she felt insecure, Jo-Jo would sit beside it and express her desire in the muted squeaky tones she employed on the rare occasions when she spoke at all. When water was added to a suitable level, she would drink happily. Henrietta, the venturesome one, would not deign to ask for help in such a case, but would perch on the bowl's edge in an unbelievely awkward stance, putting one front foot all the way down into the water to brace herself against the bottom while she slaked her thirst. At the end, she would stay atop the bowl long enough to withdraw the wet leg and shake it several times as if in disgust, then hop down and stroll away. Not infrequently wet pawprints appeared on games or coloring books left lying on the table. Apparently fishy water was great to drink but not acceptable for bathing.

By the time the fish bowl had become a spider house in our next home, Henrietta was no longer with us—added reason for me to prefer the memory of earlier days in the bowl's career to its current status. I don't remember how long we kept spiders or what prompted their eviction, but whenever it was, the bowl went with them. It was an occasion for great, if silent, rejoicing on my part. In my mind's eye, I choose to remember a bowl of happy goldfish with a cat or two lapping water from the top.

Yes, We Have No Tomatoes Today

Dogs, especially big ones like Newfoundlands, are not usually dainty eaters, but Kasam's voracious appetite was in a class by itself. Triggered by the cortisone she was given for allergies, her urge to eat was at the root of some of our most treasured memories of her long and very special life. Not often amusing at the time, indeed frequently scary in their potential to do real damage, many of the appetite-induced events became amusing in retrospect. Top honors in my mind go about equally to the rye-bread episode, involving my mother-in-law and her dual prejudices against frozen food and non-New-York-City bread, and to the tomato episode.

I am a tomato freak. I eat them at least once a day, year round, usually for breakfast, which many people find a bit odd, but then my usual breakfast is somewhat unconventional. In late summer and early fall, when the harvest is at its peak, I'm likely to indulge my tomato tooth at every meal. At that season, I also try to squirrel away some of the bounty to help sustain me during those periods of the year when even the best fresh specimens taste like plastic imitations.

Of all the ways to preserve tomatoes, the one that I believe comes closest to retaining the essential essence of the fresh flavor is sun drying and then packing in olive oil. A barely warm oven can be substituted for the sun and with results almost as good. Jars of the dried product packed in a top-quality olive oil will keep as long as two years in the freezer and do much to help bridge the seasonal gap.

Plum tomatoes are best for drying—they have more pulp and less water for one thing, so a larger proportion of the original quantity remains after drying—but other kinds will do. One year a friend, whose garden had simply exploded with produce, gave us about a half-bushel of the variety he'd grown. They were very small, barely twice the size of cherry tomatoes, but very flavorful. After downing perhaps half a dozen for breakfast and realizing that even a tomato maven like me could never use them up before they spoiled, it occurred to me to try drying them.

The prospect was dismaying, however—there were literally hundreds of the wee red globes, and each one had to be dipped in boiling water, peeled, cut open, seeded, and drained before the pieces could be dried. It was a late August day, exceptionally hot for our corner of the world, and I had a full slate of other jobs to accomplish that day, so I temporarily shelved both the drying plan and the tomatoes—out of Kasam's reach, of course. Don came home for lunch, and when I mentioned my thought about the tomatoes, he said "Let's do it. I've got two hours now, I'll help." I'd barely organized things for us to start when an involved business call came through for me, and he ended up doing almost all the tomato prep alone.

When I hung up I found him, stripped to the waist, in a kitchen filled with steam, oozing moisture himself, quite like one of the ripe tomatoes. Almost every available inch of counter space was covered with tiny half-spheres of peeled, seeded fruit turned upside down on acres of paper toweling. The effort had been monumental, and he had to race to shower and dress in time for his afternoon appointment. I assured him I could take over the drying process.

One look at the quantity and at the bright, hot sun beating down on the deck convinced me to bypass the oven and do these the real way. Every cookie sheet and rack I had was soon filled, and I had to improvise with cardboard, aluminum foil, and string, but soon the pans of tomatoes were arranged in a long row on the bench of the deck—soaking up the sun as they yielded their moisture to the clear, dry air. The aroma was intoxicating, magnificent.

The possibility of marauders had crossed my mind, and I cast an eye around for danger. The deck is a full flight of stairs above the ground, which slopes sharply down from the front of our house to the back. A railing and gate at the end where the steps lead down keeps our dog in and others out. Cats could get through but never had—it would take an intrepid feline creature to trespass on a Newfoundland's territory.

The tomatoes looked safe enough if I kept 'Sammy (Kasam) away from them. To that end, I lined up the deck chairs along the bench, backs blocking access, tipped one table up at one end of the row and another at the other end, and ordered 'Sam into the house. She stretched out meekly on the tiled hearth—a favorite spot in hot weather—and was soon snoozing. I was just about to go downstairs to my office (taking her with me, of course), when the phone rang. I answered it around the corner of the hall in the bedroom. Big mistake.

The call was brief—but not brief enough. Looking back and checking against the time it had been when I was ready to go downstairs, I calculate 'Sam had had under three minutes. The precise moment I headed for the phone—an action she would have predicted at the first ring, having learned long before that such an event often opened the golden door of opportunity—she must have headed immediately for the tomatoes.

Hired workers should be so methodical. She had gone under one tipped-up table and pushed the chairs enough to squeeze through (without making a sound) and had simply inhaled the tomatoes like a living vacuum cleaner. One half of the last rack—with perhaps twelve or fourteen small pieces of succulent fruit—were out of her reach behind the tipped-up table at that end. It was that table falling as she tried to finish the job that alerted me.

I knew before I got to the deck what had happened, but I still had trouble believing the sight of all those racks, scarcely disturbed, only one tipped half off the bench, but utterly empty except for a dozen or so pieces at the end where the table had fallen. One small piece of tomato was on the floor. 'Sam dove for it as I let out some sort of half-strangled cry, and then she slipped quickly past me to flop contentedly on the hearth, for all the world like an innocent bystander.

I was furious and I was frustrated at my helplessness to undo the deed, but most of all I was devastated at the prospect of telling Don what had been the end of all his hot, hard work. It was a dreadful afternoon. I straightened the deck furniture, washed and put away the racks and pans, tucked the few remaining tomato pieces safely into the oven to dry, and tried to brace myself for the forthcoming confrontation.

What to say? How to tell him? How to make him know how sorry I was for his wasted effort? How to apologize for letting it happen? (What to do with 'Sammy? He never had hit her, but I couldn't blame him if he felt like belting her, yet I'd have trouble bearing it if he did.) At last the poor unsuspecting guy came home, so smiling and grateful to be out of the heat and into his comfortable house that I took one look at his happy face and burst into tears. Out spilled the story in a heap of words.

For one long moment, Don looked as though he'd been hit square in the midsection. He literally wilted in stunned disbelief then very slowly turned to give 'Sam (lying quietly on the hearth) a long, level look and said, with monumental calm, "Let's hope they don't make her sick."

These days, when we think of our darling 'Sammy who is long gone from our lives, we are likely to speak of the time Don peeled and seeded hundreds of tomatoes for her afternoon snack.

And, no, she was not even slightly sick from the feast.

Playing Fair

It seems to me that people who enjoy cats more than dogs are looking for entertainment more than for love. Not that cats are unaffectionate—they can be very loving, indeed. Whenever *they* want to be. Dogs are dependably loving, willing even to be roused from a nap or diverted from any other activity for a cuddle, and never, never (well, almost never) resentful at being summoned or being ignored, according to their masters' whims.

Cats, on the other hand, are generally far more entertaining—to watch. Perhaps it is their very independence, their "Don't-call-me-I'll-call-you" attitude toward physical contact with people that makes them so playful. Romps between friendly cats are standard, reason enough for many folks to keep a pair or more as pets, but to me, the best of all are their solo clown acts. As is true of human clowns, it takes a great deal of underlying grace and control to produce the superficial clumsiness that makes their acts amusing. Only an accomplished dancer, skater, or acrobat can do the gawky routines and take the awkward spills we love without looking foolish instead of funny.

Everything is a toy to a cat. A crumpled piece of paper, a bit of string, or the classic tangle of yarn—all become living prey to be watched, stalked, pounced upon, batted and tumbled, and ultimately vanquished in an endless display of feline physical virtuosity. Paper bags, even a crack ajar, are secret caves to enter and conquer with great stealth, erupting at last into a fury of rustle and hustle, and usually ending with a mad frenzy of flight. Furniture becomes a range of mountain peaks to be scaled as though pursued by, or pursuing, the devil himself. Narrow spaces are immediately seen as tiny challenging chinks in the armor of some fortress of other—to be squeezed through with caution and cunning. Anything that rolls—a ball, a grape, a pebble—is transformed instantly into a living, breathing beast that must be subdued with full vigor. Even in the absence of a single object that can be pressed into use as a toy, a cat that feels the urge to play, *will* play. A sliver of dancing light, a shadow, a speck on the wall will do. And they manage to carry it all off with no loss of dignity. Even their flips and flops and stiff-legged leaps are accomplished with grace and charm. They manage somehow never to look foolish!

With dogs it's different. One could almost feel sorry for them! Oh sure, a cluster of puppies is adorable to watch as they rough and tumble and do mock battle with each other. And few actions are as classically funny as a puppy going full tilt in pursuit of its own tail. They look foolish but we love it. Adult dogs, though, that chase their tails with any frequency are considered to have a "vice," a bad—and somewhat sad—disorder. Professional animal behaviorists are frequently consulted for help in correcting the canine tail-chasing habit. It seems that cats, for some reason, have won our approval to continue childish absurdities into adulthood or even old age.

Maybe dogs sense our human ambivalence about their play, because most seem to take an interest in toys or games only if people are playing with them. Our Samantha may have been part cat or a case of retarded development for she was a true clown. Never pretty, ungainly and awkward to the point of being pitiful at times, she nevertheless continued her kittenish approach to life as though to say "If you are embarrassed at my behavior, that's your problem—I am what I am, and no apologies."

She loved to play with people but also played alone, and she never outgrew toys. Like human children, she generally got more fun from household items than from purchased playthings. Her absolute favorite was an empty milk carton. One day, I had tossed one at the wastepaper basket and missed; it hit the floor and bounced once, and Samantha was on it in a flash. Her foot landed on the side causing the carton to spin and shoot off at an angle, skittering across the floor. She whirled after it, pounced again, it skewed off in another direction—and the game had been invented.

Forever after, any time she could beg one, she would chase a milk carton—sometimes for nearly an hour—and eventually rip it to shreds. But there was no doubt at all that her intent was to keep it "alive" and bouncing and scooting and spinning as long as she could. With great deliberation, she would avoid coming down on it squarely, to keep from squashing it and ruining the bounce. But she also seemed to catch on quickly to the fact that, if it got somewhat bent and dented, it would take wilder leaps and turns—and be twice as much fun.

I got tired of picking up the scraps each time she finally did one in—and I got tired of cleaning up sprays of tiny milk droplets from everywhere (until I got smart enough to rinse the carton thoroughly before I tossed it on the floor!), but, try as I might, I never stopped feeling guilty if I simply pitched an empty milk container in the trash.

Sometimes I have wondered how often friends of mine or of the kids came into my kitchen and saw bent and mangled milk cartons strewing the floor and were never told why. We had grown so used to them that I have no doubt we often forgot to make even a half-hearted apology for the mess. Now and then I would remember to say "Sammy's toys" as I kicked one aside and led a guest to the kitchen table for coffee or a snack.

Samantha had other toys. Balls intrigued her from the first, but her jaws were so powerful that it was only after she had destroyed almost every kind and type of ball we or the children owned that we got bright enough to buy a special one for her. It was advertised as "indestructible," and that was no misrepresentation because it actually outlasted Samantha and her mighty mouth. Years after she was gone, it remained, the bright red faded to a dirty beige, the surface chipped and poked where she sank her teeth to catch and carry it and sometimes lie down to work it over with a deadly chewing force. But it held up more as though made of steel than of the dense hard rubber it was.

The ball felt almost like steel too—two and a half inches in diameter, it was so heavy that many dogs could not have picked it up in their mouths at all. Some of our other Newfoundlands did, but many tried and gave up. Either their jaws would not open widely enough or the weight was just too much. Samantha used to *throw* it. She loved to have a person toss it for her to chase and capture, but, if no one was around, she would pitch it herself, with a sideways snap of her head. We used to watch and laugh at her confusion when she appeared at times to have no idea which direction it might have taken. *We* never could fool her—she kept her eyes steadfastly glued to the ball and would race to its predestined spot the moment it left our hands—but she fooled herself. Or pretended to.

By that time, "The Ball," as it became known, had been banished to the outdoor pen—an essential step to protect furniture, walls, and windows—but, when we first acquired it, Holly and Deb had taught Samantha a hide-and-seek game. Sam had just graduated from a beginner's obedience class (which I, as her handler, had barely survived), and the girls used her "Sit," "Down," and "Stay," training in the game. One of them would take Samantha into the dining room, and, with her facing away from the living room, put her in the sit or down position, show her the ball, then order her to stay while they hid the ball somewhere in the living room. The person who had given the stay command would then go back, release her, and tell her "Go find your ball." In the beginning, the ball was not actually concealed but just placed next to a chair perhaps, or against the wall under a window. As Samantha eagerly bounced into the living room with Holly or Deb, both girls would keep encouraging her to *"Find* your *ball"* and direct her here and there, pointing to the ball when she seemed to be looking at it and clapping with delight if she approached it. She loved giving pleasure and caught on quickly to the fact that they were both ecstatic if she ran to the ball and grabbed it.

Soon, the ball was really hidden—half under the skirt of a chair cover in the early stages, then in increasingly more concealed places. One favorite hiding place was in the magazine basket—quite a few magazines got torn as Samantha dug for the buried treasure—and another was under a sofa cushion—a snap for Samantha to tip up and out of the way. She would play the game for as long as people involved would keep going.

It was not long until Samantha had to be stationed farther away during the hide portion of the procedure, for she quickly discovered that, without moving from the commanded position, she could turn her head and watch through the archway that led to the living room. Sometimes, one of the girls would stand with her hands over Samantha's eye while the other person placed the ball. After The Ball had been exiled from the house, other toys, even other balls, were used, but Samantha seemed always a bit confused and unsure of how to play the game with a substitute quarry. It just was not the same.

Sammy loved to chew and inevitably destroyed some items not intended as toys, for which she was soundly scolded. We tried always, when we would discover her chewing on a no-no, to apply sound child-rearing principles and hand her an "okay" to replace the forbidden object. That got to be a challenge because she could destroy almost anything in just minutes. We had bought her rawhide—she treated it like dog biscuits, once devouring every shred of the largest, knotted piece available in less than two minutes—and the so-called indestructible nylon bones lasted only a few days.

We also tried real bones. Now most bones are simply not acceptable as either food or toys for dogs. People who don't believe that have never heard or read of the dogs that die, or live only after painful and expensive medical intervention, from splintered ones. At the very least, there's the risk of broken teeth.

However, we had to find something Samantha could exercise her jaws on, so we went to a butcher and got the largest, hardest beef knuckle bones we could find. Given to her raw, they sometimes withstood her assault for a week or so before chips began to crack away, at which time they were discarded. We didn't always notice in time and finally abandoned the entire bone effort as too dangerous. But there was a curious twist to that story. One day, I saw Samantha out in the pen chewing vigorously on an unidentified object. I sent Deb to investigate, and she came back with a small round bone, the kind with a hole in the center that is a crosswise slice of a long bone such as the one in an animal's leg. This one was about the size of those found in one kind of beef pot roast, no more than an inch-and-a-half in diameter and perhaps three-quarters of an inch thick. It was not new. Bleached to near whiteness and polished like a stone from a running brook, it looked almost like porcelain.

We had no idea where it had come from. None of us had given it to her or seen it before. We could only assume she had dug it up from a spot where it must have resided for years—long before our yard was fenced. As we examined her precious possession and tried to figure out how she had come by it, Samantha bobbed and bounced and wriggled and squirmed, obviously beside herself with the fear we were about to keep it from her. We were. Or, we intended to. She was giving off signs of such acute distress and such unbearable longing that we could not. I decided to let her have it for awhile but to watch carefully for signs that it was beginning to disintegrate and then to remove it permanently. I never had to. Whether she, incredible as it seems, was "careful" of it so it would not crack or shred, or whether it had been all but fossilized by a prolonged seasoning in the earth is hard to say, but she cherished it for years, and it never had to be taken from her. Nor, I think, could it have been, except by one of us. It was the only object she would not let the other dogs share. None ever tried to tamper with it more than once.

No dog we've had since Samantha loved toys as she did. Kasam never played with anything. She would prick up her ears briefly at a purchased squeaky toy as though wondering what made that odd noise; she would give a sniff or two at one of the kinds that are supposed to smell like meat or cheese, and then walk away as though in disgust at an unfunny joke; and she would follow a rolled or bounced ball once or twice as though vaguely curious about what it might do next, but that was all the interest we could arouse. She would not retrieve a tossed stick, would stare at a knotted sock thrown across the room as if wondering what had come into us, dropping our clothing about so casually. She *ate* rawhide. She didn't suck and chew and mouth it for fun or exercise—she simply ate it as rapidly as she could, swallowing such huge chunks whole that we worried about intestinal stoppages and ceased giving it to her.

Shauna does have moments when she loves to play—but only at long intervals. A pair of socks tied together and an old bath mat knotted in the middle intrigue her now and then. She will pounce, grab, toss, chase, chew, roll on her back and lift such an object above her face and catch it with her mouth, and sometime leap with all four feet in the air at once in the sheer joy at her own antics. The fun will last anywhere from three to ten minutes, prompted by no situation or event we can identify, and then will cease with equal abruptness. After one such wild fling, it is likely to be weeks before she gives the toy another look.

The only game she seems always ready for is her version of "fetch." A rubber boat bumper is her favorite. Any of us can toss it for her out-of-doors and she will break all speed records to pursue, capture, and return with it. But then the game switches to "keep away"! She approaches, stops, wags the tail, but when the human playmate reaches for the bumper, she dips, twists, and runs a few yards off. Pursuit is what she wants, and if the person will play, Shauna leads them on a merry chase round and round, feinting, stopping, eluding capture at the last moment, diving under the picnic table, zipping behind a shrub, racing toward—and then on past—her pursuer, even stopping at times and depositing the bumper on the ground in front of her. "There, I'm through, you can have it," she seems to say. But as a hand gets within inches, she pounces once more and takes off on another round of tag. Sometimes the bumper is held firmly crosswise in her mouth but other times, she grabs it by the end and it flops around like a giant cigarette from the corner of her lips.

Shauna plays the game fairly though—by her rules. She never cheats. If a human hand can actually get itself to the bumper, whether it is on the ground or sticking out of her mouth, she yields instantly and stands, waiting for it to be thrown again. Tug-of-war is *not* part of the deal. Her game is simply a contest of speed, agility, and strategy. Her former owner, who had used the bumper to start training Shauna for water trial work, would be horrified at my letting the entire retrieve exercise be ruined this way. But, I am never going to have the energy and stamina to carry on with the formal training; it is something I always wanted to do but lacked first the opportunity, then the time, and now the vigor. Meanwhile Shauna and I both get some needed exercise at the game that has evolved. And we both have fun. What could be more important?

Toys meant little or nothing to most of the other Newfies who have lived with us. 'Sicha's fun was in the run and especially in the hunt—she loved to stalk and catch small rodents, snakes, and even a pheasant once. She presented a weird sight sometimes with the snakes she caught—running proudly, head held high, with a three- or four-foot specimen writhing and twisting as it arched out from both sides of her mouth. It would have looked utterly comic if one could have stopped feeling sorry for the poor snake's predicament.

Bitches that had had litters generally reacted to proffered toys as though they were sluggish newborn puppies that had to be licked, tumbled, and otherwise stimulated into breathing, sucking life. Luckily, most real pups responded and did as expected quickly enough to avoid the mauling that inanimate objects were likely to be given, as efforts to arouse them were increasingly stepped-up in response to their nonresponse. Shalom, our huge, gorgeous male must have had his hormones slightly askew (indeed, he so thoroughly sabotaged all our plans to make a stud dog of him that, more than likely, his male hormones *were* out of whack) for he treated toys much as the bitches did. He destroyed more than one of the childrens' stuffed animals, doing everything he could to make them move and live. We would find soggy masses of fabric and filling—no tooth marks or intentional tears to be seen but pummeled and mouthed to the point of disintegration. Several times we caught him in the act, and his entire demeanor suggested frantic, *loving*, frustration as he cuddled and licked and rubbed and rolled the furry bundles.

Much as Deborah and Holly fumed at such destruction of their prized critters, those losses were small compared to the time Shalom loved (or "mothered") to death a real creature—Holly's pet guinea pig. One of the beautiful, long-haired fluffy kinds, the guinea pig lived much of the time in a cage in Holly's room. She took him out frequently and he scooted around exploring corners and other objects. During those free times, he had encountered dogs—always under Holly's supervision—and had not appeared overly concerned at their sniffing and pushing at him with their noses. On the other hand, he didn't seem overly thrilled at their attentions and tended to crawl away from their continued attentions. All the dogs, including Shalom, had been exposed to the guinea pig, and all had wagged their tails and acted quite benignly.

One evening we were all away. As was usual whenever we were out, at least one dog was left in the main part of the house—this time it was Shalom. We came home to find him in the room next to Holly's, guarding a wet, limp mass of fur and flesh that turned out to be a very dead guinea pig. When we picked it up, Shalom seemed so anxious, so distressed, that we could only believe he thought we would somehow manage to revive it. One of the friends that had come home with us was a doctor—a pediatrician—and he helped us examine the lifeless body. There were no lesions, no wounds, no signs of maltreatment other than the wetness of saliva.

Ken's verdict: a heart attack brought on by fright. The familiar phrase "scared to death" took on new meaning.

The guinea pig had been left in its cage, of course, and we will never know whether it got itself out or whether Shalom had loosened the latch of the cage. No matter which one had initiated the "play," it was a sad and deadly game that time.

Perhaps the most amazing thing is that, with all the animals we had over the years, and the diverse species that frequently shared house room, there was only one other episode in which one pet did another in. Many years before, a parakeet we had was killed by a cat and, though that may have started as a game, there was evidence to suggest it might have turned quickly into something less fun for both of them. Behind that feline façade of grace, of play, of kittenish charm, lurks the tiger still.

Bishop-in-Residence

Holly was not quite eight years old when Bishop Berkeley came to live with us. This Bishop was a pet hamster that tried hard to live up to his famous name by repeatedly posing near-insoluble dilemmas, but Holly's choice of name for the tiny rodent was probably not based on a presentiment of his escapades. More likely it was simply a reflection of my conversations at the time, heavily laced those days with material gleaned from the writings of the original Bishop Berkeley, one of the philosophers I was studying. We all pronounced the hamster's name in the British way, "Barclay," just as the great philosopher's was.

Bishop, the hamster, spent a good deal of time out of his cage, being carried here and there by Holly, often running about on the floor or play table near her, sometimes poking his head inquiringly from inside her clothing, where she had tucked him. He took many field trips with her: out-of-doors, to friends' houses to play and even once to first grade, where he was smuggled in by pocket and removed to display for "Show and Tell." Nights (and most school days) he spent in his cage. His inordinate amount of freedom, however, led us into several harrowing experiences. He even caused me to make my "first mistake."

Holly was taking piano lessons and generally did her practicing before school, on the enclosed sunporch off the kitchen, at an old upright we'd bought second-hand (or perhaps tenth-hand) very cheaply. To try to minimize the instrument's monstrous ugliness, we'd painted it to match the wall it leaned against. Several coats had been applied to mask the chipped, dark veneer, and when a piano tuner had come to work on it, we'd had difficulty getting the upper panel open so he could get at the business part of the insides.

While she practiced, Bishop usually climbed on Holly's shoulders or scurried back and forth across the ledge where sheet music was propped. This had gone on for weeks with nothing more untoward happening than Bishop's occasionally dropping onto the keyboard, adding a little extra discordance to Holly's less-than-polished efforts. But perhaps he was getting bored with the routine.

As I cleared the breakfast things one morning and Don and Deb scurried around getting ready to leave the house, Holly's playing came to a crashing halt. That was followed by a wail that may well have disturbed the human Bishop Berkeley in his grave. We all converged on the scene where Holly pointed to the narrow opening behind the music-rack panel and informed us that "Bishop went *in* the piano."

We pulled the panel out as far as it would go, got flashlights, peered, and poked, but to no avail. From the sounds inside, Bishop had gone down and was in the lower bowels of the instrument somewhere in the vicinity of the foot pedals. Holly called and coaxed (against all logic, he did sometimes seem to respond to her commands) but no small body appeared. He either *could* not or *would* not climb back up to where he could get out.

While Holly alternately wept and demanded corrective action and Don tried to think of a solution, I announced in my usual pessimistic fashion that the jig was up, there was no hope, Bishop was doomed. Don tried to pacify both of us by announcing that he would remove the front panel below the keyboard and try to get to the poor creature from there. Determined to maintain my crêpe-hanging stance, I proclaimed in the most absolute terms possible

(Berkeley the philosopher, as well as my professor, would have given me an F for adamancy, if not for effort, had they heard me) that after all the paint jobs it had had, nothing short of axe work would separate that panel from the rest of the piano.

While I continued to foretell doom in strident terms, Don pried with a knife blade at one edge of the panel, and, even as I spoke, it popped off with the greatest ease. Out slipped Bishop, unharmed and frisky as ever.

Suddenly I was aware of Holly's eyes, riveted not on Bishop whom she had calmly scooped up and was cuddling in both hands, but on *me*. The look on her face was strange to behold, but before I could attempt to interpret it further, the scramble was on to make up lost time and be off to school and work.

The answer to the look on Holly's face came two days later when she brought home the current issue of the weekly "newspaper" her class put out. The lead story was hers. It told of Bishop's escapade in the piano and ended with the awesome pronouncement that "So, for the *first* time, my mother was wrong!"

How had I fooled her so long?

To this day, whenever I make a mistake of any size or kind, one of the kids is almost certain to counter with "Mom is wrong— that's the *second* time." Bishop made a few more mistakes too, but I'm not sure whether anyone kept accurate count of them either.

Counting the Cost

An Irishman I once heard speak said that horses are so important to the folk of the Emerald Isle that, if it came to that, a family would give their own breakfast to their horse—that no Irish horse could starve unless its owners did. I do not know if that is true, nor do I pretend to judge whether such an attitude makes sense, but I do understand the feeling. Our children's food was never taken from their mouths to feed the dogs, but their carefully hoarded savings, from birthday gifts and extra chores performed, were wiped out to help buy Samantha, our first Newfoundland puppy.

Contributing those savings was the kids' own idea, nor was it the last time they volunteered to help scrape together cash needed for canine-related expenses. Even Don's father, who scarcely knew the difference between dogs and horses (and in the case of Newfoundlands wasn't too sure there was any) was called upon to help—when we realized we had to buy a car for Samantha.

Looking back one has to wonder at our stupidity in not recognizing the problem sooner, but puppy love had really played havoc with our normal clearsightedness. Little Samantha, the puppy, came home with us in our tiny, compact foreign car, nestled quite snugly and comfortably between the two kids on the back seat. In the months that followed, she rode most often with me to the veterinarian, the grocery store, all around town, on the back seat of our old Plymouth sedan. And then one day it became groaningly obvious we had a problem: there was no way we could get the four of ourselves *and* the dog in either vehicle for a planned visit to friends twenty miles away!

As a result, ages before we had meant to or could really afford a new car of any kind, we bought a station wagon. We had not thought, before Samantha, to own such a vehicle. Nor was that to be the only time our choice of kind, or time of purchase, of transport was determined by pet needs. Years later I was driving an old Jeep wagon well beyond the stage where it made economic or comfort sense and even beyond what our mechanic warned us was a dependable safety level, because it was the only vehicle our aging and precious Kasam could get into and out of. (Alas, we were aging at the same time and could not lift even her relatively slight Newf-size.)

Earlier, when she began having difficulty climbing into the tailgate of our other car, Don had cut the legs off a stool to serve as an intermediary step. For a couple of years the stool stayed in the back-back of that car to be used whenever 'Sam got in or out, but one day, her failing eyesight caused her to step down on the edge of it, it tipped, she went face-first into the gravel—and would not trust that contraption again.

When the back seat of the Jeep was folded down and the side door opened, 'Sammy could get herself in and out by feel and familiarity. What she lacked in grace she made up for in enthusiasm, for she loved to go—anywhere. She always seemed so peaceful in the Jeep, in spite of the jouncing and bouncing as we tootled along, and when I left her there to go in and out on my errands, she would snooze happily while I was away and wake up to kiss me each time I returned. So, we kept the ancient, rusty Jeep, bought it new tires, prayed that what had to be fixed could be, and that it would hang on as long as 'Sammy did.

It was a sorrow—a minor one to be sure, but a sorrow nonetheless—that 'Sam's last trip was not in her beloved Jeep. That journey, which we did not at the time know would be the final one, was to a specialist fifty miles away, and we were afraid to do it in the old Jeep. We managed to lift 'Sammy into the other car, trying hard not to damage her dignity too much. Coming home that day could scarcely have been much harder for us than it was, but probably would have been worse yet had we been in the Jeep with no Kasam behind.

I drove the Jeep one more time—to turn it in for salvage. Its usefulness was gone when 'Sammy was.

Most breeds of dogs do not cause changes in lifestyle and budgeting of that magnitude. They do have needs—most of all, love, and that is free—but love does not fill an empty stomach or shield the recipient from weather and disease.

Probably everybody today assumes they must provide food for pets, but that was not always so. The dogs we had on the farm when I was a child were expected to forage for themselves, existing almost entirely on rabbits and other small creatures they caught, only very rarely being tossed a scrap from the table. In those deep Depression days, *we* ate just about every scrap ourselves and supplemented our own diets with wild creatures such as rabbits whenever we could. The cats (none of which ever came in the house) were totally on their own, except when they could sneak a lick or two of warm milk from a just-emptied pail. Even today, cats seem more able to scrounge for their food, if they must, than most dogs, although many of the more delicate house-raised ones might not know what to do with a mouse if one wandered by.

Pets' need for shelter is, alas, less well recognized. You can hear otherwise-intelligent-seeming people insist that the animals are naturally equipped to withstand weather. Humane officers, veterinarians, and biologists—along with sensible laypeople—know that is utter nonsense, and they also know the practice of leaving dogs out of doors with no protection from wind, rain, and temperature extremes is downright cruel. In some climates and at some times of year anywhere, there is no need for an elaborate structure—a lean-to or a nook under a porch may be adequate, but shelter of some kind is essential. Indoors with the family suits most pets best of all.

It does seem to me pointless to have pets if they are not in the house to be enjoyed, at least part of the time. Dogs bred strictly for work—herding sheep, for instance, or hunting—may be more in the nature of livestock and housed accordingly with some logic. In that case, the animals are not pets at all, although they must develop a good relationship with their handlers if they are to be good at their jobs, so I imagine the people spend a lot of time outdoors.

Weather is perhaps the least of the environmental dangers. Protection from other perils can be even more critical, because statistics show the average life expectancy of a free-roaming house pet is less than *one year*. The primary threat is vehicular traffic, but other hazards exist too: bones and toxic materials ingested while scavenging, injuries from fights with other pets or wild creatures, parasites and illness-producing organisms picked up anywhere and everywhere, and damage inflicted by people who are annoyed or frightened by dogs. No matter how smart a pet is (or its owner thinks it is!) it can not protect itself from such dangers. Pets must depend on their owners to provide safe ways to get exercise. For some breeds, brisk walks on leads are sufficient, but the larger and more active kinds need room to run vigorously. Unless one is fortunate enough to have an absolutely secure private field or beach, fenced enclosures are the only answer. For people in apartments that may be impossible, which means their choice of pets is severely limited.

It amazes me that communities spend the sums they do creating recreational and sporting facilities for the public—golf courses, beaches, boat launches, tennis courts, and all manner of parks, bridle and bicycle paths, hiking trails, and playing fields—yet, never have I known of fenced areas set aside for people to exercise their dogs. Surely there are more dog owners per capita than there are tennis players or equestrians. Clean-up is, of course, an issue to be dealt with. But scoop laws are at least as enforceable as regulations against other kinds of littering, an ongoing battle in all public areas. The first time I hear that horseback riders must gather up their mounts' deposits, I will get more concerned about dog owners who neglect their clean-up duties. Given appropriate areas for exercise and the needed equipment to do the job, I believe dog people will be at least as responsible as the general public. It must simply be that pet owners have not seen fit to speak out regarding their needs.

Good food, exercise, and protection from hazards go a long way toward keeping a pet healthy. But medical care at some level is also a must. With luck, little beyond vaccinations and checkups will be required—at least for years. Eventually all animals—if they escape sudden, accidental death—fall victim to the ills that accompany age and the wearing out of a body's parts. Some less-fortunate ones, like their less-well-endowed human counterparts, have on-going or massive medical problems that can run veterinary bills into the thousands. To date, pet health-insurance plans have not been structured so they appeal to most owners; perhaps that will change.

Except for the wealthy few, I doubt there is a logical way to determine whether or not a person or family can *afford* pets. Costs to buy and to support the animals vary so much. A high-quality purebred puppy of one of the more expensive breeds requires an outlay far beyond what other puppies go for. Both are considerably more than the modest fee asked by most animal shelters, and adopting an otherwise doomed cat or dog brings its own special rewards.

One of the smaller breeds is obviously a better choice for people on a limited budget than a Newfoundland, Great Dane, or St. Bernard—a toy poodle certainly eats less than a Newfie but, surprisingly to many people, not that much less. Newfs tend to be lazy and, left to their own devices, spend far fewer calories per pound than a frisky terrier that races from room to room and up and down over the furniture for hours each day. A kennel owner once told me that a healthy golden retriever or setter or hound, given the exercise it needs, eats more food than a non-working Newfoundland.

Small dogs don't have special vehicle needs either, although they too enjoy the back of station wagons because they can see out without standing up at a window. They should have crates for riding in the car though. Less secure than the shoulder-lap belts for people, a crate nevertheless provides some protection if quick stops are called for. The safari type generally work best for car travel because they allow free air circulation and much more visibility than the more enclosed kind. One of each kind is even better—one for the car and the other for the house. A crate is a wonderful training device, and a dog left at home alone tends to be more contented in its crate, once the space has become a familiar nest. The house and furnishings are likely to stay in better shape as well!

Difficult as it is to come up with an accurate estimate of the cost of having a pet, it is even harder to reckon the value of the benefits. For some people, pets literally make the difference between lives that are worth living and those that are not. Reports abound of elderly, ill, and lonely people of all ages whose only pleasure, only reason for being, is the sharing and the loving they gain from their cats or dogs, even birds and other creatures. Scientific evidence increases daily of the solid, sometimes startling, physical, mental, and emotional health benefits that accrue from relationships with animals. Such values cannot be measured in dollars and cents.

Sadly, some of those who need pets the most desperately find it difficult to meet even minimal costs. The companionship of a loved and loving pet can do much to alleviate the loneliness of older people, especially those who have no spouses and few friends and whose ability to get out and mingle is reduced by health problems. Yet those are the people who often must get by on very limited budgets. High on my personal list of charities is an annual contribution to an organization that helps supply food and medical care to pets of elderly people in financial straits. I can think of few expenditures where a small number of dollars can do so much.

We did not always feel so charitable toward prospective buyers of Newfoundland puppies that we had raised for sale. In fact, we found ourselves quite impatient at times with families that came to tell us how badly they wanted a Newf but that they simply could not pay the price we were asking. No doubt that was sometimes true, but, too often, these were people who had not found it at all impossible to own a television set (about the same price as a Newfoundland puppy), to hook up to the cable (about the cost of feeding a Newf in most communities), to have the machine repaired when needed (often comparable to veterinary bills), and then to replace it with a new one when it no longer functioned (probably after a shorter life span than a well-cared-for dog might be expected to enjoy). If I could not afford both, I would choose to own a Newfoundland rather than a television set; for me the pleasure to be gained would be greater and more dependable.

On several occasions we gave away dogs, for absolutely nothing, but those were unusual circumstances. Once we gave one to a hopeful breeder who had had bad luck investing more than he really could spare in bitches that turned out to be unacceptable for breeding. Plenty of less-conscientious people would have bred them anyway in an effort to recoup some of their losses. He would not compromise the breed that way and, when we had a promising female puppy with no purchaser on the horizon, we let him have her. Later, when she had produced two good litters, he was to pay us. Alas, his miserable luck held and she also proved to be displastic and unbreedable.

The other times we gave away dogs—adult animals in each case, with special needs—we did it for what we thought was the good of the dogs. We lived to regret one of those in particular. Perhaps we were just poor judges of character, but I am inclined rather to agree with breeder friends of ours who insist, somewhat cynically but probably accurately, that people take better care of something they have put some of their hard-earned money into than they do a freebie.

No matter how high the price seems to be for a pure-bred puppy, buyers can generally rest assured the sellers are not getting rich. Except for the conscienceless puppy-mill operators, breeders are not likely to even make up their costs. It would be better not to tell the IRS perhaps, but breeding dogs can hardly be considered a business; most of the breeders we've known whom we respect view their activities more in the nature of a serious and expensive hobby, with puppy sales helping to defray the expenses incurred.

Some people who tried to convince us that owning a Newfoundland was their fondest dream but one that was unattainable because of cost had spent far more on a host of things that they obviously found more rewarding: golf clubs and tennis racquets (you can get a lot of exercise with a dog if you want to and both will benefit); boats and skis; club memberships (it is amazing how many convivial people you can meet walking a dog or going to shows); power tools and other craft equipment (you can feel the pride of your handiwork when you take your well-groomed, well-trained dog out); cameras, fancy cars, adult "toys" of a thousand kinds.

There is certainly nothing wrong with expenditures for fun and leisure. All but the most pinched budgets should have slots for some of that. Man—nor woman, nor child—can live life fully without some investment for pleasure. "You pays your money and . . ." but the choice is free.

An Ice-Cream Tail

Enticing food, left within easy reach of a dog, is likely to prove too tempting for even the most well-behaved pet. But Kasam, one of our otherwise trustworthy Newfoundlands, developed her skill as an out-and-out food thief into a high art. Seldom out of sight for more than a minute or two, 'Sam learned to make those minutes count, although the speeds at which she ingested her loot meant she could scarcely have tasted, much less enjoyed, what she stole.

I eat breakfast alone and always read while I do. One day, as usual, I prepared my plate of food, put it near the toaster on the kitchen eating bar, which is regular counter height. On the plate was a typical (for me) breakfast: sliced hard-cooked egg, wedges of tomato, some cream cheese, and chunks of other cheeses. Matzos were in the toaster oven, ready to be warmed, and a mug of steaming coffee sat at hand. As I prepared to enjoy that, my favorite meal, I noticed there were only a few pages to go in the book I was reading. The comfort I take from my breakfast routine doesn't bear interruption well, so I thought it best to have reserve reading material on standby.

It took me no more than twenty steps each way to the living room and back, and I swear that sixty seconds could hardly have elapsed, but I returned to an empty plate in the kitchen. Empty!

The coffee sat in place, steaming away, the matzos were warming in the toaster, the nearly completed book sat placidly on its rack, and the plate was no more than an inch or two out of place. 'Sam lay on the floor where I'd left her.

A small smear of cream cheese was all that proved the plate had not been taken clean from the cupboard. Nothing else remained. The exact moment I left the room, 'Sam must have lifted her forepaws, very gently, to the edge of the counter from where she simply sucked up every bite of food on the plate, with nary a scrape or rattle to betray her action, and then to have dropped quietly to her former position on the floor before I returned.

Several years earlier she had had a much longer time to perform her deviltry, but had left the scene almost as devoid of clues. That was in the early days of her drug-crazed appetite, when we had not yet quite caught on to the depths of its drive and sometimes left her alone in the house for a few hours.

One such evening we returned to find everything apparently in order, praised her heartily for being such a good girl, and went to bed. No problem. The next day, however, as I moved around the kitchen, something nagged at me, from the corner of my mind as it were. Suddenly it dawned on me. The fruit basket, which sat on the kitchen counter, was empty. Of course, sometimes it was, but this time it should not have been. Indeed, it was with a jolt that I realized I had put a good-sized cantaloupe in it two days before to finish ripening. I was also sure there had been at least a couple of apples, and probably some oranges or bananas, in there as well.

My first sensation was of shock. Someone had been in our house! Cantaloupes and other fruit don't evaporate. What else was missing? I raced around the rooms looking for other signs of disturbance or thievery but found nothing out of order. And not a *trace* of the missing fruit. Don was unable to shed any light or offer any explanation (I had wondered if he'd had a manic-sized craving for fruit at midnight perhaps), and the mystery persisted for another day or two. Until I moved the dining room chairs to do a thorough vacuuming job.

Far under the table was one apple stem, five or six melon seeds, and a small yellowish stain on the carpet. The only conceivable explanation was that in our absence, Kasam had had a feast of fruit. In the dining room, of course. Clearly, such treats deserve appropriate surroundings.

We will forever wonder *how* she did it. How did she remove the fruit—especially a whole cantaloupe—from the basket without knocking the basket to the floor or even tipping it over? (Or did she pick the basket *up* and put it *back* on the counter??) How did she get the melon into the dining room? By rolling it? And how did she eat it—rind, seeds, everything—so neatly that only one bit of juice and a few seeds escaped? And how did her intestinal tract handle that orgy with no obvious rumble or flip? She never revealed her secrets.

Like most kids, though, she had a penchant for not doing what was expected. We took this—the ultimate chowhound—to a Newfoundland fun get-together one Saturday, sponsored by the local breed club. A series of delightful contests had been devised for the pleasure of the assembled owners and their Newfies. We entered 'Sammy, then almost ten years old, in a few of the competitions, but our hopes for taking home one of the attractive trophies were pinned on her winning the ice-cream-eating contest. In fact, we felt the others were wasting their time as they lined their animals up and held them, sitting in a row as directed, along one side of the host family's driveway. Other members placed a row of paper plates, with equal, measured quantities of vanilla ice cream on them, a few steps in front of the dogs.

At a signal from the stop-watch holder, the dogs were released, each to have a go at the nearest plate of ice cream. Nineteen dogs pounced, slurped, and gulped, many sending their plates flying as their tongues went for the cold sweet stuff. Well—not nineteen, actually. One demure canine lady first sniffed hers appreciatively and then proceeded to lick around and around it, carefully, daintily, like a well-bred person dealing with an ice-cream cone, oh, so slowly, savoring each small taste. Kasam.

She finished last.

I can only think that *permission* to eat something so delectable allowed her to revel in the experience and make it last as long as possible.

She may have sensed our disappointment though, because she won a prize for me that day after all, taking a first in the tail-wagging contest that wound up the affair. The trophy, a lovely leaded-glass Newf-head silhouette, still hangs on our mantel. And in our memory, 'Sammy's tail has never stopped its sweet, rhythmic wag.

Big Trouble

When our cat, Jo-Jo, died at the age of seventeen-plus, we were, for the first time, a felineless family. Jo-Jo had been one of two kittens Don and I had taken to live with us shortly after we were married. In her lifetime, two children had arrived, and many pets had come and gone. Henrietta, Jo-Jo's litter mate, had disappeared when Deborah, now finishing high school, had been four-years old.

Twinkle, an enormous neutered tom who joined our family for five years or so, had always belonged more to place than to people. When neighbors of ours, who owned him, moved a few miles away, Twinkle refused to stay moved. He kept returning to his former territory and, after making repeated trips to collect him, that family finally left him with us. When we moved, it seemed best just to hand him on to the people who bought our house and who wanted him.

Jo-Jo's primary canine sibling had been Ginger, a beloved mutt who lived twelve years before succumbing to the ailments of old age. Soon after Ginger's departure, we acquired our first New-foundland, Samantha, only six-weeks old but already out-sized. Jo-Jo managed to hold her own, nevertheless; her age and wisdom served her well in establishing authority over the rowdy youngster.

The truce that was struck early between the two held even as Samantha grew into monstrous and vigorous adolescence, and a wary sort of friendship developed between the mismatched pair during the short remainder of Jo-Jo's life.

As Samantha grew—too much, too fast, and too "crooked"—it became clear she would not become the breeding stock we had hoped for. If we were to begin even the small-scale kennel we envisioned, we would have to acquire at least one more Newfoundland. Quarters were somewhat tight, there were zoning laws to consider, and my time was thinly stretched as I had resumed full-time work outside the home (to help support our budding breeding hobby!), so when Jo-Jo died, my response to requests from the children for a kitten, was an unequivocal "no."

Unequivocal it may have been, but that didn't stop their endless efforts to wear me down by pushing me to justify my stance. Even the argument that Samantha, and other Newfoundlands to come, would try to play with a kitten and surely *kill* it in the process failed to still the pleas. Particularly urgent demands arose because the cat of a friend of Holly's was "expecting." (This was the same family— as nuts as we were when it came to animals—who had nearly done us in with their gift of black "white" mice a few years before.) The pregnant cat was gray and white, the sire was known (they swore) to be a big orange fellow from next door. Both were beautiful, both nice pets, etc.

I listened but I refused to be swayed. Once, however, exasperated beyond good sense and tired to death of using reason and logic to no avail, I leapt way out on a limb and said "Sure. Okay. Fine. We'll take a kitten—if it's *black*. We are starting a Newfoundland kennel, and *all* animals we have from now on must be *black*."

"And female," I added.

The words were scarcely out of my mouth before Holly was on the phone to her friend to relay the good news that she could have one of the kittens! "A black one," she remembered to mention, as an unimportant detail. The bargain was struck and Holly was beside herself with glee. As the days went by and I heard her telling everyone she would soon be getting a kitten, I began to be ashamed of myself. No way that litter would include a black baby. (What a lot I didn't know about cat genetics or feline *affaires d'amour*.)

As the pregnant cat's time approached and Holly's excitement grew, I pointed out as gently as I could that it was very likely there would be no black kittens. I also took care to mention that black *and* white, stripes, spots, and such wouldn't count. "I mean *black*—like Newfoundlands are black," I reiterated. Holly listened and went her merry way, preparing to own a cat.

It was very early Sunday morning, Mother's Day that year, when the friend called to say the cat was about to give birth and Holly was invited to watch. Leaving me to enjoy Mother's Day morning in peace and quiet, Don took Holly to witness the great event.

My blissful return to unaccustomed morning slumber was short-lived. The ringing telephone, scarcely half an hour later, was no more disruptive of my equanimity than Holly's voice announcing triumphantly that the first kitten was born—and it was *jet black*. It was, and it was the *only* black one out of a collection of seven. All the others were the expected variations of the gray-orange-white theme. Not only was that first kitten really black (I did check on the possibility of a dye job, but the black was genetic and permanent) but it turned out to be a "she," tipping those fifty-fifty odds solidly in Holly's favor. A few days later, I made one last stab at recouping my loss by discovering and pointing out a splash of white on the black kitten's chest but had to make my final retreat when Holly reminded me I'd said the kitten had to be "black—like a Newfoundland" and that Samantha had a white patch on the chest. She did, as do many other black Newfs.

When that tiny sooty feline creature was weaned and came to live with us, I fully expected disaster and lamented, as the kitten entered, "This is *big trouble*." It was, for Holly promptly named her "Big Trouble," and she was our welcome and cherished B.T. for the next sixteen years. The expected disaster never came. Samantha was as careful of the tiny creature as if it were her very own baby to nurture and protect.

After such an infancy, B.T. grew up to be about the most unflappable cat one could imagine. She moved twice with us, adjusting with absolute ease to new houses and outdoor territories; she saw the children grow up and leave; and she lived with and outlasted about a dozen adult Newfs and quite a few litters of puppies. It's not usual to lament the lack of trouble, but we still wish we could have our Big Trouble back.

Beware the Dog—Maybe

Once, shortly before midnight, in a poorly lighted and very *un*nice area near the riverfront in Trenton, New Jersey, I found myself taking Shalom for a pre-bedtime bathroom opportunity, while the rest of the family were asleep in our nearby motel. Such activities were usually taken care of considerably earlier, and, in such surroundings, Don—or both of us—would normally have undertaken the chore. We had travelled all day, though, and schedules for dogs as well as people often get skewed under those circumstances. So, after trying unsuccessfully to talk Shalom out of his mood, I had dressed, snapped on his lead, and gone out.

Our mission was accomplished with due dispatch some two blocks from the motel entrance, and we were on our way back when a group of young male persons appeared on the sidewalk, roistering their way toward us. I believe they had been sitting, mostly hidden from view, on a bus-stop bench near the motel.

At first glance, I thought there were a dozen. There were, in fact, four. Enough. They were in a mood to have fun and, although the 180 pounds or so of heavily coated black dog facing them may have caused some inward pause, they seemed terribly eager to outdo each other in their outward displays of strutting masculinity.

When they first materialized, directly ahead of us, I had moved with Shalom to the far left of the sidewalk, close to the building, and continued along our way. As we neared the group, Shalom—properly trained though he was to stay on my left—simply defied the rule and crossed in front of me to place himself on my right, between me and the oncoming noisy crowd.

I had an instantaneous flashback to life with Samantha, our first Newfoundland. She used to drive us crazy whenever we tried to respond to a doorbell or a knock; we always had to stretch completely across her large body to open the door, and even the dearest friend or most frequent caller had to postpone a hug or handshake until Samantha decided to move aside and allow entry. In almost every case, her tail was furiously wagging and she literally smiled in happy anticipation even before the door opened, but, no matter how pleasant she seemed to expect the encounter to be, she put herself between the caller and her family until she was sure.

Or, was she just determined to say hello and get a greeting herself before we took over the visit? I've never been sure.

None of our family and none of the Newf owners we know has ever found out what exactly one of our beasties would do if a real confrontation occurred. And it really doesn't matter. Because the other person doesn't know either. If an approaching person has malice in the heart, wouldn't the mere presence of such a sizeable unknown be restraint enough for most?

I do know there's an awesome amount of power packed into the body of a full-grown, healthy Newfoundland. People who see them at work—dragging fish-laden nets in from the sea, hauling sledges piled high with logs, or pulling the inert body of a half-drowned person through icy water and raging surf are made stunningly aware of their capabilities. People who live with them as pets, however, are seldom exposed to the potency of their force. Oh sure, one swipe of a tail can clear the coffee table, and being catapulted down the sidewalk on the near end of a leash attached to an untrained Newfie is a pretty good clue. We have had a few other demonstrations as well. In the hard-to-believe-my-own-eyes category was another Samantha episode: One day, I hooked her to a wrought-iron railing in a schoolyard near our house while I supervised our children and some others, at play. Something happened—at this late date I have no idea what it was—but Samantha perceived it as danger.

Once, twice, I saw her leap at her tether, only to be stopped short by the half-inch-link, welded-steel choke collar she wore and by the iron railing, which was imbedded in concrete. I yelled something at her—intended to reassure her there was no cause for alarm—but she did not trust my judgement. As I watched, she gathered all 160 pounds of herself into a knot of power and, with one enormous lunge, was free. She did not hang herself. She did not break her neck or separate her head from her body. She did separate two of the links of her collar. No doubt it was the proverbial weak link that gave way—some welding job inadequately done—but the mind-boggling part was that, when we picked up the pieces of the collar, the link that gave way was not just cracked apart but changed from an O to a wide-open U. I have the link still, among my Newfie souvenirs.

I for one, do not care to find out what it would be like to see such strength aimed in anger at a person. I shudder at the thought of a Newf that would intentionally do harm to a human being. Sadly, I must admit I have heard reports of kennels that produce Newfoundlands capable of hostility to people—I do not even like to hear about such creatures.

Yet, one of the most-often asked questions, and one that has always made us uneasy when posed by a prospective buyer of a Newfoundland puppy, is "Are they good watch dogs?" The answer is easy: No. Period. A standard joke is that a burglar who enters a Newf's house will be greeted by a wagging tail and be led straight to the best silver or the jewelry cache. Many Newfoundlands rarely even bark, especially in the house. We've never had one that did except at passing dogs or other animals, and I'm inclined to think those occasions are friendly "hellos" rather than any kind of warning. Shauna shrieks when our doorbell rings! But what she objects to is the raucous, piercing sound it makes, not the person pushing the button. We know because we've tested it: if one of us steps outside and, with the door open and in full sight of Shauna, presses the bell, she screeches. If someone knocks or, a close friend or family member, simply opens the door and steps in, Shauna runs to say hello—but silently.

No—it isn't the answer to the watch-dog question that poses a problem—it's the asking of it. Threats to life and property are all too current in today's world, regardless of where or how we live, and it would be senseless to resent people's urge to feel more secure. Yet, I believe it is wrong to look to dogs for the security. True, certain individual animals of certain breeds can and are trained to assume potent roles as protectors of people and property. Such training and such roles may be justified—even necessary—in specific situations, but I don't like it. I am much happier to see those functions assigned to inanimate objects—alarms, fences, and, where and when needed, weapons—all controlled by and backed up by thinking human beings. Besides, people who are looking for a dog to guard and protect are not looking for pets, and pets were what we were producing.

Newfoundlands have a long and proud history beyond petdom, as working animals, but their work has always been to help their people by doing physical labor, never through inflicting damage on another human being. Nor through inflicting damage on other four-legged creatures either. The Irish and Russian wolfhounds, for example, have a noble heritage along the latter lines—and they are to be respected for it. But Newfoundlands are not like that. Or shouldn't be. Most Newf owners, and all the reputable breeders that I know, agree. The single most important specification in the current breed standard—the official document that spells out the ideal Newfoundland—is "sweetness of temperament."

Some of the folks who ask about Newfies' protective tendencies might think that that "sweetness" has been carried too far. I suspect more than one would be inclined to call them wimps. Sometimes they are wimps! Calm and placid and unflappable as most of them seem to be most of the time, we've seen a wimpish side of just about every one we've shared life with. It can be downright comic if a bit embarrassing, to see one of those huge beasts turn into a quivering mass of black fluff. Which is about what a spooked Newfoundland looks like.

It happened even to Samantha. Her first Waterloo was the entrance to the clinic at the Cornell College of Veterinary Medicine where we took all our creatures for medical care during our Ithaca years. She would not enter the waiting room. Naturally, it occurred to us at the outset that she was expressing her unwillingness to be on the receiving end of the kind of activity that went on in that place. Not so. Once inside, she was happy and content, even delighted with the attention, never seeming to notice, much less object to, shots and all such. No—it was getting in there that stopped her cold.

To do so required going up a flight of gray granite steps and across a small foyer. The stairway and foyer had been added onto the outside of the building and enclosed completely in glass. When Samantha was only a puppy, we hauled and dragged and boosted her along to get her up and in. Because she was half-crippled with displasia (an all-too-common affliction of many breeds, including Newfoundlands), we thought perhaps the stairs were just too difficult for her. But, as she grew and learned to negotiate stairs elsewhere, it became clear there was more to the clinic problem.

Early on, she would go part way up, sometimes nearly to the foyer landing, before planting her feet and then turning tail to hurl herself (and whoever was holding the leash) back down. Time and again we tried. We tried coaxing. We tried bribing with biscuits. We tried commands issued in our sternest voices. Students assigned to clinic duty came to our aid, but, short of picking her up bodily, they didn't succeed any better. As she approached 100 pounds around six months of age, the picking-up-bodily system ceased to be an alternative.

One day, when we had to abandon all efforts, even with strong, young help, a student suggested he go up and through the clinic to open the *back* door, normally used as an exit, for us—it gave onto the side of the building atop the slope so there were no stairs. He thought, with enough help, we could push and pull her through there. Good idea. And it worked. But not one whit of pushing or pulling was needed. When the door opened, she literally raced inside, happy and eager as always to "go visiting"—to see people! From then on, we would call ahead and arrange for someone to let us in the back way for Samantha's medical attention.

So—what was the problem? We finally decided that it was some confluence of the elements of shiny floor, glass, and height. As she neared the top and saw what may have looked to her to be an unwalled area, above the ground, she thought she was going to be led off the edge? Or did the light pouring through the glass on the polished gray stone look as though there was no floor at the top? Whatever it was, she was literally terrified of it, and even having gone the route (against her will!) on several occasions, she was not reassured.

Years later, our theory about the problem appeared to be verified, this time with a less happy ending. We had built a new house, and with no such intention—indeed, without ever thinking about it—had produced almost a replica of the clinic entrance. The house was on a slope with the bottom floor at ground-level on one side and partially below ground on the other. The entrance, on the high side of the slope, gave onto a foyer about midway between floors. From the foyer, some eight or nine steps led down to the ground floor; five steps went from the entrance up to the main level.

The first time Samantha was let in—via the dog rooms which were at one end of the lower floor—she bounded, in her always-clumsy but generally effective manner, with great eagerness and joy, all the way up the first set of stairs to the foyer-landing, made the turn to go up the rest of the way—and balked. Stopped cold. Whimpered. Started up again. Made it to the second step. Whirled and leapt back to the landing. Stared longingly at us—now gathered at the top. Tried again. Then turned and fled, all the way to the ground floor. Holly went down, petted her, calmed her, took her collar and saying "come," quickly led her up again. To one step beyond the landing. That was it. She would go no farther.

Several times we got helpers and carried her up. She wanted so badly to be up there with her people. Bedrooms (and dog rooms) were on the lower level, but the top story was where the action was: kitchen, living room, dining room, etc. It's where her family was—unless they were asleep. It was where company was. It was where other dogs often were. It was where fun was. But she was terrified to tackle that second set of four or five steps up. And she was never completely comfortable up there even when she'd been carried up.

In the beginning, we thought—and hoped!—the problem was temporary, but one day I had a sudden memory of the clinic entrance of yore (it had long since been remodeled to eliminate the stairs), and the similarities hit me like a cold Niagara. There they were: shiny, light-colored floor at the top of steps and a wall of glass, floor-to-ceiling, straight ahead. Through the glass, tree tops and sky. No evidence of terra firma outside from that vantage point. How awful! In her own house. Cruel fate.

Poor Sammy. She never did learn to handle it. We tried many things—dark blankets on the floor at the top, night-time when the glass wall became, to us, a black blank, everything we could think of. But the fear was too great. We gave up at last and spent more time with her downstairs and outdoors and riding in the car to try to make up for the banishment from the normal family get-together times, but I do not think she ever stopped longing to be up there with us.

Or—did she worry about us, living in such constant danger of falling off, falling through, or whatever? Who can say?

Lots of dogs are not happy with shiny floors, perhaps because they can be slippery. We've had temporary problems with three dogs on the kitchen floor in the house where we now live. Each of them stopped short the first time they came to the doorway and were reluctant to step off the carpeted area onto the polished wood. (No walls of glass, no stairs, just smooth, shiny floor.) But, with coaxing, they did, very cautiously and gingerly, step onto it and all quickly accepted it as no problem.

Nothing much bothers Shauna—after all, as an unusually large female with a near-perfect physique, it's hard to imagine why any ordinary thing or creature would faze her. But even she met her match; she came totally unglued in the presence of a Newfie puppy twelve weeks old! The first time she encountered Holly and Pete's little Charlie, he weighed less than twenty pounds, came only about to Shauna's elbow, and was nothing but a bundle of happy, friendly fur. When he looked up at our great beast and reached his nose out to say hello, Shauna literally leapt in the air, gave forth with frantic yelps (Get away! Help! Help! Oh Lord!), and fled for her life. It was simply hilarious—to everyone but Shauna, who nearly took a storm door off in her panic to escape.

Other wee dogs don't have that effect at all. For years she has been the best of friends with Holly's Rusty (a tiny little mixed-breed) and Deb and David's two little critters—not one of which weighs even a dozen pounds. She neither runs from them or at them—except when she plays "race-dog" with Deb's wee Bichon (who outruns her with ease). Cats, including our two, are dear friends. Why does Charlie spook her?

Someone in the family suggested that maybe she is scared to death that whatever caused Charlie to shrink down to that insignificant size might happen to her. "Little dogs that are *supposed* to be little are okay," said the wise-acre, "but a midget Newf is scary."

Well, maybe that's not so crazy. It does remind me of the one time our huge Shalom was reduced to jelly and of our surmise about his thoughts then. We had chosen Ganshalom as our kennel name. "Gan" we understand to be a word for "garden" in Hebrew, so the name meant "Garden of Peace," or "of Love," or of other benevolent connotations of the word "shalom." (In our less romantic musings, it was simply "Shalom's Yard"!) Our house sat at the end of a longish driveway, mostly hidden by shrubbery and trees—easy for visitors or delivery people to miss, so I commissioned a young couple to construct and install a sign that would be both informative and decorative. It was a silhouette, in wood, of a standing Newf, about five feet high and perhaps six-and-a-half feet long from tip of nose to crown of hanging tail. Painted black with brass letters spelling out "Ganshalom" across it, it made a handsome and, we thought, welcoming motif at the end of the driveway near the road.

A few days after it was installed with rods implanted in the earth and a brace behind to keep it upright, I strolled out the driveway with Shalom on a leash to take a walk up the road into the woods and fields. He loved such outings and was prancing eagerly along at my side until suddenly, as we were about to make the turn into the road, he spied that thing. He reared back, he crouched, his eyes rolled wildly as the hair stood almost straight out over his whole quivering, shivering body. I could not believe his obvious terror. It was a riot. Maybe my burst of laughter was the last straw; something, anyway, seemed to trigger a spurt of testosterone, because he did, very quickly, recover his manhood enough to stand his ground.

I stopped laughing, I petted him, he eyed the thing, I talked soothingly, he watched it warily, but little by little, he let me inch him toward it. It took awhile, but he finally did give it a thorough going over (including, at last, a lift of his leg on its hind leg) and, when he relaxed, we were able to pass.

He never took that darned sign totally for granted—it was always in his sights as we went past—but he came to believe he had it cornered. We all decided it had simply shocked his socks off when he first saw it because, by golly, by gee, there was a Newf bigger than he was.

Then too, the sign didn't walk toward us as those young men on the Trenton sidewalk a few years later were doing. That night, his first reaction—to step to my right and body block—was soon inadequate, as the oncomers left us no room to pass. Forced to stop (or push our way though, an option I rejected), I drew in the leash so Shalom was tight against my knee. Again, he defied his obedience training that required him to sit whenever I stopped, and remained standing—quietly with no outward reaction to their absurd performance. That performance now included loud comments on the dog's size and questions directed to me about what he was, where we were going, what he eats, and such nonsense, all accompanied by pantomimes of fear and other expressions of mock dismay. They clowned. We stood.

At last when things were beginning to get a wee bit tense, one of their number reached out a tentative hand toward the placidly standing Shalom and gigglingly asked, "Is he friendly?" I caught a note of sincerity underlying what I believe he meant to be a jeering tone, so I looked straight at the young man and said "As long as you are friendly to me, he is friendly to you." The reaction was comic: eight hands went simultaneously heavenward, as four voices in near unison proclaimed "Oh, *I'm* friendly!" Four bodies moved aside and we walked peacefully on. They *had* been afraid. I'm sure of it.

Of course, they didn't need to be.

I think.

When Newfies Last in the Dooryard Bloomed*

I have a rose garden. Well—*we* have a rose garden: Don takes care of it; he feeds and waters the plants and gives them their shots against disease and bugs; I just look at the blossoms and love them. He enjoys them too, but he also likes begonias and fuchsias and dahlias and tulips—every bit as much as he likes roses. Not me. All those other flowers, and many more, are delightful, but they just don't play in the same park as roses, to my mind. This is no claim to fame on my part. Most of England and probably at least half of the rest of the world seems to agree with me. Even Gertrude Stein.

I have to disagree with Ms. Stein on one thing though: A rose may be "a rose, is a rose . . . " but in my garden, each one is an individual, and more than just a rose. Each plant of mine has two names: the one the grower assigned, and another I have given it to stand in memory of a dog I've loved and have no more.

Several Peace roses are in my garden—surely they are among rosedom's brightest stars—and they grow there in living memory of our own "Garden of Peace," our kennel, Ganshalom. Shalom himself—the rose I call by his name—stands sentry along the walk

*With apologies to Walt Whitman

just beside the front door. It's a huge and sturdy bush. Pruned back every January to a few stubby, bare-bone stalks, it grows to nearly six feet tall by late summer. Some of the canes are as thick as my thumb, the foliage is lush and dark green, and it turns out dozens of impressive blooms of the deepest, richest, reddest red you can imagine.

The blossoms on another bush show that same incredible red—on the *inside* of each and every petal. The outsides of the petals, though, are a pure and snowy white, as is the heart of the flower where the petals are still curled shut. *Regal* is the only word I can think of to describe it. And regal, indeed, was our Becky gal. A queen in bearing and in beauty, in behavior (some of the time!), and in her achievements that earned her places of honor in the Newfie record books. Her name, which is part of the pedigrees of so many super dogs—of which Shalom was one—is my name for that royal rose in our garden.

A salmon pink blossom seemed just right for Samantha. Not only the flower—which is not exactly the prettiest rose I've ever seen!—but the shrub itself that always seems to grow in a lop-sided, loose-jointed way, and the foliage, which is all too susceptible to disease, are appropriate as a memorial to the crazy, crooked clown she was. And, like Samantha, that rose, on close inspection, surprises you with its sweetness. It pervades its surroundings with a spicy, cheerful pungency.

Shir Hashirim—"Song of Songs"—is at one corner. From three feet away or more, it looks like a rather plain white rose. One must come very close to see the soft pink blush that floats like mist among the petals, a heart-tugging reminder of the lovely Shir that passed through our lives so briefly like a rosy haze. So delicate. So fleeting. Was she there? She must have been—our precious Kasam was one of her puppies.

The wild and zany runaway, the flamboyant, irrepressible, too-big-for-her-britches, great-fun-but-exhausting-to-live-with 'Sicha blazes away at one corner. The shrub is low and squat but well-balanced and tightly knit. The flowers bloom in binges—a dozen buds forming and opening at once and staggering the viewer with unreal splashes of bronze, orange, gold, and flame, all intermingled in each and every flower. Then it just shuts off for awhile before starting up again. Ah, what a reminder of that little scamp.

Other roses are there in my garden also—one for Tari and another for Melech and for Littlest Angel. Probably more are still to be added. I do hope it will be many years before we plant a Shauna; when the time comes, though, it will have to be a magnificent yellow one.

Near the center of my garden stands the choicest rose of all, the one that seems to express the essence of Kasam. The plant itself is a beauty and the blossoms are glorious. They look marvelous growing there or cut and clustered in a vase. All alone. They would mix and blend with others if asked to, but their loveliness is too enchanting all by itself to bear diluting. An odd and special color, described in the catalog as "creamy ivory with a blush of soft pink and traces of pale apricot," the grower dubbed it "Summer's Dream," I think. I might suggest a less poetic, but no less delicious, description: scoops of vanilla ice cream with drizzles of peach or apricot jam. And what a heavenly scent. Now there's a rose. Now that is a rose 'Sammy would love—perhaps to eat. Why not?

Friends and neighbors, who know not its extra meaning, have told us they enjoy our garden. Just as our friends and neighbors have enjoyed our Newfies. Strangers sometimes stop to look and to make comments, which, their smiles tell us, are pleasant ones. Just as strangers used to pause outside our Ganshalom fence and smile and point and speak of what they saw.

For us, the garden is a special welcome home. Whenever we return—from a three-week trip, from a morning full of errands, from a five-minute walk in the neighborhood—there they are, all our kids from days gone by, smiling their sweet hello. They are not gone.